The Voice

a Spiritual Approach to Singing, Speaking and Communicating

... making revolutionary knowledge from the past available today ...

Miriam Jaskierowicz Arman

The Voice: A Spiritual Approach to Singing, Speaking and Communicating

ISBN NUMBER 0-9674181-0-0

Printed in the United States of America
October 1999

All drawings, including cover, are the original work of
   Miriam Jaskierowicz Arman
Editor: Penny Phillips
Cover and body layout and design: Kerry Phillips

To my mother, Mila Jaskierowicz, with love, devotion and gratitude.

dedication

This book is dedicated to the memory of my beloved daughter, Aviva Hope Bershaw, who left me much too soon on Thanksgiving Day, 1996.

A few days before she died, she made me promise her that I would write this book. Because her life was dedicated to helping and giving to others, she wanted me to share what I know with generations of singers yet to come.

She loved until the last moment of her young life, and in that love I found my peace and my strength to go on, to teach, to write and to continue my work. Her life enriched so many others, and it was her wish that my life does the same. I promised her this work and with it, I rededicate my life through these pages to being the best teacher I can be and to give of myself to all those who seek my help.

I love you, Vi! Please sing a melody for us with God's angels.

I also dedicate this book to the memory of my beloved father, who gave me courage and strength to fight for what I believe in and whose life and personal integrity illuminates every day of my existence.

And finally, there are the voices of Six Million, who never had the chance at life, who burned in gas chambers, singing "ANI MAAMIN - I Believe," while being lead to their deaths.

May my work be a tribute to their memory and to those beautiful and talented members of my family, my grandparents, aunts and uncles, who perished, just because they were Jews.

acknowledgments

I wish to thank my students in all parts of the world who have worked with me, respected me and loved me. To them I am grateful, for without them, I would never have found all the guidelines outlined in this work. Their generosity of sharing their thoughts with me, their allowing me into the deepest crevices of their souls, their opening to my constant and endless questioning and their permitting me to enter the sanctuary of their voices has taught me beyond measure. I am deeply grateful to all the spiritual guides that have chosen me to impart their knowledge to the singers who enter my life.

Thank you. Muchas Gracias. Grazie. Toda Raba. Spasiba. Kozemem Sepen. Danke. Merci. To the outstanding Maestri with whom I have worked, who have allowed me into their studios and assisted me with my singers. A thank you to all of the wonderful talents that I have not had the pleasure of meeting, to those who will buy this book, who will understand it and create their destinies with it.

Most of all, I thank God for having guided my way into this work. A hard and trying, often tragic, road filled with tears and strife—but always giving me the strength and power to carry on, loving every moment of every day. I thank Him for my ear, for my feelings and my instincts; for having given me this marvelous gift, which I promise to value and cherish until the day I die. I evoke His blessings for this work and pray that my life will be the source of light to those who will want to find it in the night.

Miriam Jaskierowicz Arman
September 1.1999

table of contents

preface

I could tell you many a story that's occurred since I began writing and rewriting this book. They all would lead to only one conclusion: this book had to be written. Many times I was apprehensive and wanted to turn back because I thought of what others might say and how they might react. But then the voice from the inside strongly objected and said, "What are you afraid of? You know what you have done is good and those you have sent on their way have given you the right to share this knowledge. It does not matter how others might feel or how they might judge. Take your stand and open yourself up to the world."

I have said many times throughout the book, and I want to do so here at the beginning, as well: There are many teachers in the world with just as many ideas and theories on how to teach. I respect their dedication and their efforts. This book is not meant to take anything away from them, or to refute or challenge what they are teaching. I am not in competition with them. I have very simply outlined what I teach, how I teach and what has been helpful to so many students all over the world. I share my work with all those who wish to partake of it.

I have been involved in teaching 18 years, and my life has

been enriched by the students I have taught and by the beauty of their voices and their beings. I have had the great pleasure of touching many lives at various times in my career, who have in turn shaped my very existence to the core. Through the pain and the heartache, it is the voice—the beauty of the instrument, the perfection of its creation—and the devotion of my students that bring me to this point. I care deeply about you—the singer, the professional speaker, the communicator in all of us—and hope that this work serves as an enlightenment to each and every one who comes in contact with these pages.

Miriam Jaskierowicz Arman

"We create our tomorrows by what we dream today."

"You are the sum of your thoughts and feelings, plus or minus... positive or negative."

"If you can dream it, you can achieve it; and if you can wish it, it can and will be yours."

"A singer is only as great as his last performance."

These are some of the phrases I use in the beginning lessons. Teaching is not only the knowledge of the voice, but also the proper application of a great deal of psychology. The more positive your attitude is in your life, the easier you will be able to assimilate the information.

As a teacher, I build a bridge between my students and myself; and that bridge enables us to communicate in such a way that our experience is one of love, sharing, lots of work and ultimately—accomplishment.

 In the Beginning

In the Beginning

Once upon a time, there was a little boy playing with old and dusty things in the family attic. In a far corner, he detected an oddly shaped black box and went immediately to check it out. To his great surprise, he found the box in pretty good shape on the outside—other than the mildew and the dust, of course. But the big amazement came when he opened up the case. Underneath the beautiful, red velvet lining, he found a lovely looking violin, which seemed to have been polished only yesterday—a bow, strings and other strange looking things... he had no idea what some of them were. "Wow, what a find! I wonder how much it's worth?" he thought to himself. Immediately he decided to pay a visit to the old bearded man that owned the music store down the street.

None knew exactly from where the old man came, or how long he had been there, but the little boy remembered that sometime long ago, he had seen a violin hanging in the man's window, and he had admired it. So, with the black case in hand and dreams of riches, he headed off to the shop.

When he entered the music store, he heard wonderful sounds. The old Victrola in the back was playing, and the small store seemed filled with the delicious tunes of piano and voices, violins and flutes. The little boy just stood there for a moment, taking it all in. What a strange and enchanting place.

The old man smiled at the boy with his wise, blue eyes and beckoned him to the counter. "Well, well, what do we have here?" he asked. "Oh," said the little boy, "it's a violin I found in the attic... so I thought I'd bring it to you and see if it's worth anything and if it's still okay."

The old man opened the case, removed the velvet covering that lay neatly over the violin, lifted the instrument out of its case and gently placed it under his chin. Then he took the bow, tightened it and began fingering the strings and adjusting the neck of the instrument. He knew exactly what he was doing; and he did so with love, smiling all the while, enjoying himself and this adventure. The little boy watched in wonder. "Perhaps one day I, too, will play the violin," he thought to himself.

The first sounds the instrument made were kind of squeaky, harsh and unmelodic... sort of hard on the ears. But all at once, as though something magical had happened, the violin started to sing. Beautiful tones began on the top and continued to the bottom, creating a haunting melody... resonating throughout the store. The old man's eyes lit up like two light bulbs, and a great smile played across his lips. "This is a fine instrument," he said. "Yes, a very fine instrument." "Is it valuable?" asked the little boy. "I mean—if I sold it—how much money can I get for it?"

The old man sat down and said, "My dear young friend, the value of the instrument is not as important as who is playing it. In the hands of someone who doesn't know how to play it, the instrument is worthless. But in the hands of a master, a very plain *Woolworth* model turns into a *Stradivarius*.

And so it is with the voice, the greatest instrument of all. As we begin on our path together, it may seem arduous and a bit difficult at first—because it's unfamiliar—but I promise you that very shortly, you will understand everything about the voice and will be glad you chose to become a "master."

The violin cannot be played in its case. It has to be taken out and put in the proper place for playing. Only then can the master create beautiful tones and melodies. Well, the same thing applies to the voice.

Let us then begin together, taking your *instrument* out of its case—or box—and endeavor placing it where it belongs. You will find that your conceptualization of where the voice lives, from where it comes and how to use it will drastically change. That is my mission.

I must tell you first of all, that I am writing this book because of my passion for the voice, for my students and for the state of the Art as a whole. I am one of the most fortunate people in this world, who wakes up every morning excited about the day—about the discoveries I will be making and the joy I will experience… the sharing… the love that is in my life. I give myself completely to my passion and, as my students will tell you, I live my life to its fullest capacity.

I am a purist… I abhor spectacle for the sake of spectacle. I love the performance, but I am not a lover of mega-concerts—nor do I believe in the sound systems used to make them possible. I want to hear the voice, the pure sound, the beauty, every note, every magnificent nuance.

I want to be transported by music—the artistry, the quality of the singer—not the hoopla that goes along with mega-productions. Perhaps I am old-fashioned. Perhaps I do not understand or care about the money angle of the whole thing, nor do I want to. I certainly don't believe that it should be the motivation for a performer. For me, the focus is the voice, and that's what it will always be.

Each voice is so different. Each student is so special, so individual in his or her needs, and I treat all of them that way. Each one has a magic button—a word, an action—something that will make him finally click and find the voice. Finding and understanding that magic button are the marks of a good teacher, one who loves his students and cares about their progress. Discovering the magic button usually takes time, but that is what makes the whole process so wonderful and exciting. I live for the moment in which both the student and I capture and achieve total transformation, because when it is right— you and I will feel splendid, elated, joyous, easy. You will be flying, and I will fly along with you.

Specifically, when all is said and done and everything is in place, you will not feel the voice at all anymore; it will have disappeared into the head. You will hear echoes of sounds that are perfectly placed, yet out of your control. You will make them in comfort and without effort—this is where we are heading with these lessons, and this is the place to which I will lead you: total and complete comfort without strain, force or trepidation. No manipulation. You can be completely free to give yourself to the music, the drama, the art of singing.

I have come up with specific guidelines that can apply to everyone. There are hundreds of variables in the voice, and after reading and digesting this book, each of you will begin to understand your own instrument and will be able to make evaluations that will be good for you. Read each chapter over many, many times. If you keep in mind the most basic things we are discussing here, you will do wonderfully well. I will make it very easy for you, so follow along and most of all—enjoy.

This is not a scientific book. There are no fancy terms or drawings. The few drawings I chose to include are those I draw for my students every day. They are easy to understand because they go along with the ideas I am presenting here. I want to teach you just as I teach my students. I have broken down the concepts in such a way to make it really easy for you. Expect to hear different terminology than you are used to and learn to integrate it into your own vocal vocabulary.

I have been teaching voice for many years. I have taught in Italy (as well as other countries in Europe), Israel, Hungary, Romania, Poland, the Ukraine and Russia, Slovakia, Mexico and of course, here in America. My students have come to me from many parts of the globe: Argentina, Venezuela, Belize, Brazil, Jamaica, Puerto Rico, the Dominican Republic, etc. I have had the pleasure of working with some great Maestri in Europe and have assisted other international teachers at the lessons of many a singer.

The individuality of voices always fascinates and amazes me. The artistry of singers and their tenacity and dedication to making their instruments work really intrigues me. But the countless ways the ardent student tries to produce the voice, when in reality it is already there and so little has to be done to reach utter perfection in vocal emission, utterly baffles me.

In all the years I have been teaching, I have never quite understood why we think of voice production as something so extraordinarily difficult. Perhaps the fact that it really *is* so simple is more than we can allow ourselves to hope for, much less to accept as true. How can something that is thought to be so terribly difficult really be so easy and accessible? The mystique placed on singing doesn't help our thoughts, either. After all, our famous singers are bigger than life, and to most of us, it seems hardly possible to achieve such a goal.

Does this line of thinking reflect your sentiments? Well, let me burst your bubble. It's easy. It *can* be done. And after you *have* it, *feel* it and *achieve* it, you, too, will agree that singing is such a *natural* thing—even a child can do it.

When you can not feel the voice anymore because it seems totally out of your head... When it does everything on its own, and the only thing you have to do is hear the music in your head and allow the *brain the freedom to do all the work—that is when you will know the voice.* You will hear sounds such as you have never heard before. You will experience feelings that seem surreal. You will find yourself floating in space and making music at the same time. *You will be at one with the universe!*

This is not going to be a very long book. It doesn't need to be as there is basically very little to say. But if you—the singer—**really** read these lines, everything that has been unclear regarding the voice until now will be unveiled before your eyes. I will explain it all to you in these pages; and for the first time since you've begun trying to sing or speak properly, you will fully understand how to do it right. All will make perfect sense to you. The brain must accept, conceptualize and understand all thoughts; and since the brain is the major contributor to the proper working of the voice, logic and intellect will tell you that **this**—and **only this**—is the right way.

I will repeat myself many times in various contexts, because one concept will go with another at various steps of our discovery. Primarily, that is, because these concepts must be reinforced over and over again so the brain can compute, analyze and finally comprehend and incorporate the necessary actions into its reflexive motor system. Each chapter can stand by itself and bring you right back to the beginning concepts.

What begins as a learning experience will become an entirely natural thought process. I call the whole process **brain imaging,** because once the brain can form the *image* of what we are talking about here, you will be home free. All of this requires trust, above all—and that is what I ask of you. The choice is always yours; but I know that if you let me guide you through this process, you will be successful at understanding and producing the voice.

Singers have this very special instinct of survival. I have noticed it in so many of my students. Some of the comments I hear over and over again are:

- "Something doesn't feel right… I leave my lesson, and my throat feels like it belongs in a sling."
- "I'm always horse after I leave my teacher."
- "I have studied for two years, and nothing is happening; but I *know*, I *just know* that I have a voice."
- "When I sing for a little while, my throat becomes tight: and I feel like I can't go on."

Perhaps you, too, can relate to those comments. But this instinct, which hopefully saves you from singing wrong, is the same one that tells you when you have finally encountered the right thing. Let your logic guide you and know this: **if you feel *anything*, you're doing it incorrectly. If it hurts, stop immediately.** Reread the sentence of instruction and then try again.

Please, let me say one more thing to you before we get very far into this: **I know there are hundreds of voice teachers and just as many theories on the proper way to sing. I am not interested in arguing or challenging any of them. "Live and let live"—that is my motto. I am not here to prove anything to anyone. I am simply here to share my knowledge and experience with you.** The main thing is that you wind up with a beautifully healthy and finely-tuned instrument. I envision singers who have healthy voices and communicators who can do so easily and without feeling pain. I do not "right" or "wrong" anyone else's methodology or theory.

I stand exclusively on my own.

One last bit of advice: If you are studying with a singer, please beware that you do not try to emulate him or her. His voice is his own; his interpretation of how he constructs the voice for himself is also his own. Make sure you always stay true to **your instrument**. Work within your capabilities and allow your voice to shine through, without taking on the vocal characteristics of your teacher. It's difficult, especially if you are studying with someone who has made a career or is famous or perhaps, has taught someone who is very well-known on the music scene. It is quite natural to become enamored with the sound of someone else's instrument; but please, try as best as you can to develop your own.

Here I offer you my way of teaching; I offer it to you and you alone. Ultimately, you will know if it is good for you. Let your feelings and intellect guide you. Your body will tell you by its responses to what you are doing whether it accepts or declines.

Singing is as natural as speaking, and it should be effortless. Permit yourself to experience what I put forth to you. Don't immediately judge by your past experiences. Give this a chance. Only then can you make an informed decision.

There is no mystery to the voice. There is, however, the *miracle* of the voice. Accepting this is the very first thing that must be done. Let's begin our discussion by trying to understand what our individual responsibility to the voice really is. I know that by the time you reach the last page of this book, you will sing, be happy, feel wonderful and have the stamina to continue singing for hours on end. You'll be able to reach the heights within the voice that you have always dreamed of, but never believed you could achieve—and it will be easy and effortless.

It is vital that we understand from the onset that the voice is a gift, part and parcel of all the other wonderful attributes that were given to us when we came into this world. The voice is the combination of all of our emotions and feelings, as well as our physical, psychological and mental abilities. It combines all our capabilities and asks us to bring them to life in the most natural and uninhibited manner, so as not to hurt or damage the instrument in any way.

To really tune the instrument, you must be fully cognizant of it. You must know it, love it and feel for it. You must understand all the elements involved, the way it functions and what you can expect from it. You cannot fix a car without knowing all of its parts and understanding where one fits into the other. Most of all, you must be willing to spiritually dedicate your voice, everyday anew, to the ONE who gave it to you in the first place.

I truly believe that if these prerequisites are not met from the start, there is no possibility of understanding or mastering the voice. Oh, you will be able to sing, but to really make a career for many years to come is almost impossible. To be in tune with your instrument means making the decision to truly love it, care for it, respect it, understand it and above all, to **dedicate** it.

We must understand that the voice does not belong to us. Since it is a gift, it must be cherished as one. I lost my singing voice at a very early age, and the realization that I could not sing anymore made me sad beyond belief. It was only later in my life that I discovered that destiny had chosen a different path for me. Teaching others brings me great satisfaction, and although it will never replace the loss of my own singing voice, I love every minute of it. Perhaps it is because I lost it that I have spent a good part of my life delving into its majesty. I am grateful to have been chosen as a vessel to grasp and perceive the voice and thus, to be able to help others in attaining self-expression, their destiny, passion and artistry. It took quite some time to get here, but here we are; and we're both ready—me, to make sense of everything you need to know to begin becoming proficient at using your voice and you, to experience and partake of it.

People are always amazed at how I can teach without being able to sing. Well, my Dears, that is the miracle of who I am and in the last chapter, I will share my story with you. Suffice it to say that I rarely have the need to demonstrate. Because I can skillfully communicate the knowledge I have, all concepts are clearly explained. The knowledge you will need to use the voice properly consists of the intricacies of the voice, the way it works, how the body reacts, how each note sounds when it is perfect and what is imperfect. My students understand me quite easily, and so will you. **I am a TEACHER, not a SINGER.**

Many of the ideas I put forth to you are abstract in design, but entirely applicable. This method requires that your thinking process actually changes. It demands a real leap of faith because basically, you're walking blindly—at least until this begins to make a little bit of sense. But at the end you will ask yourself, "How come no one else has ever explained this to me before?" Well, perhaps someone has—but not in a way you were able to understand. With the explanations I give to you here, you will understand.

chapter 1

Spirituality and the voice... Why?

"What does spirituality have to do with the voice?" you might ask. Well, just imagine for a moment the real power of music, any kind of music. Think of its therapeutic value; the way it can make people feel when they listen; the communication gaps it can bridge between nations and cultures; the way it can overcome you when you're in a bad mood; how it makes you feel when you're happy; the way it can send chills down your spine. Music, music everywhere... in offices, on answering machines, in the home, while riding a bike or sitting on the beach, while at your place of worship or while you're working out. The power of sound: remember it.

Music moves your spirit and your soul and your mind. It can bring you to tears—happy or sad. Whether you sit in a church or a synagogue, a Buddhist temple or a Muslim mosque, you will hear music. Music... celestial sounds we associate with God, with angels, with heaven itself. Music grabs you, enfolds you, heals you, brings you profound joy and lightens your sadness. Music is, in itself, spirituality. Through music you can achieve a heightened sense of being and become sensitized to feelings and emotions you have never experienced before.

In the last few decades, there has been an incredible upsurge in spirituality. Everywhere you turn people are talking about angels and communication with the "beyond". Their interest in the world's environment and other life forms has taken on an entirely different approach, than, let us say, fifty years ago. There seems to be a yearning within us to know more, to answer age-old questions, to find the common thread in our lives, to attach ourselves to something that is beyond ourselves. Reiki, Kenesiology, Reflexology, Hands-on Healing, etc.—all this indicates a resurgence toward the natural law of things.

The "material" realm has also taken on a different meaning in many cases. Of course, we have to earn money to economically survive in this world; but the incredible thrust of the fifties to achieve more than our parents did—this exhausting competition that the baby boomers felt—has, to a large extent, been replaced by values that go beyond the house in the suburbs, the two cars in the driveway and the "keeping up with the Jones." There is an opening within us, a need to comprehend the metaphysical and to make it part of our everyday living.

Self-help, new age, homeopathy, herbology, natural foods... all of this points to only one direction: our need to feel better— physically, mentally and emotionally. The statistics of how many people take self-help courses, read new age books and shop at health food stores has been on a steady rise for the last twenty years. This shows us clearly that our lives are changing. Our personal needs are more directed toward introspection and self-realization. Our communication skills have to change to accommodate our internal changes, and this is precisely the subject on which I want to concentrate with you. **Let your inner voice guide you ,and you will come to see the Light.**

Did you know that **speaking** and **singing** are the same? The way you speak is also the way you sing. Essentially, you are using the same system, only less of it. It's as simple as that. Your speaking voice, therefore, is also your singing voice. Most of us speak incorrectly, though. We use our throats; and even though we sound and feel scratchy and complain about discomfort, we don't do anything about it. Some of us speak through our noses, taking the entire *ring* and *point* out of the voice. Some singers may sing correctly, but speak incorrectly. The results are quite difficult to deal with and can cause quite a bit of trouble.

Some of it is no fault of our own, though. We have been instructed to "keep it down," to speak quietly, to drop the volume in our voices to make it acceptable to our daily lives.

When a baby is born, it does not know how to modulate the voice, how to make it quiet. It screams "at the top of its lungs," and if you watch, its belly pumps all the while. But very soon, all that changes. "Shhh! Keep it down. Daddy is sleeping." Slowly the voice drops lower and lower from its natural position and finds another place from which to come—the throat. We learn to speak with the throat, and so we use and abuse it all of our lives.

We totally take the voice for granted. We simply don't think about it. It is here to serve us, and serve us it does—relentlessly, day after day. It is the means by which we communicate.

Have you ever thought what life would be like without the voice? Without the ability to say the things you need to say in daily life? Have you given thought to what your life would be if you could not tell your child, "I love you" or speak words of solace to the friend who just lost his mother? What would your life be without language? Imagine yourself in silence for just one day.

Take a moment and think of how incredibly important your voice is to you every moment of every day and how lucky you are to have it in every conceivable situation of your life. Think of the pain you would never be able to express, the joy you would have to hold inside, the songs you could never hum.

From this day forward, you who are reading these lines will no longer think of the voice the way you did up until now. From today on, you will change your whole perception of the voice, for speaking and, of course, for singing. All you have to do is follow me on this path, and you will be on your way to a wonderful voice in speaking, as well as in singing.

Whether you will sing or speak professionally is really not important here. What is important is that your instrument is tuned properly and that your wonderful gift is preserved for your entire lifetime. That is my mission, and that is ultimately what I am here to share with you.

chapter 2

How do we Begin? the Breath

The breath is the lifeline of the voice. The way you breathe determines where the voice goes, and where it stays; if it remains in place, or if it falls. The breath is the motor and the support of the voice. To master it is the most important task we must set for ourselves. The kind of breath I am talking about is totally natural. It opens all the most important places. I'll be specific and give you step-by-step guidelines so you can easily follow.

1. Open your mouth slightly, not more than the **natural drop of your jaw**. Take in a very large breath from the top of your front teeth and allow the air to travel along the roof of your mouth all the way to the back. You will feel a cool sensation along the hard palate (roof of your mouth), all the way into the back of the throat.

2. When it seems that you cannot go any further with the breath, you will have arrived at the *soft palate* and the *hole*, which is the exact place where you need to be. Once you feel that, you are on the way to understanding how it all has to begin. The spot where you feel the coolness is exactly where you have to be… **the *soft palate*.** Every note, and I mean **every** note, that you

will ever speak or sing will be initiated in this same place. When you can conceptualize the movement of the *soft palate*, all the other pieces of the puzzle will fall in place quite easily. Please remember that this is only the start, and as we become more familiar with the whole system, we will be referring back to this cool spot quite often.

You do not have to worry about taking sounds *up* or *down* any more. No changing of positions is necessary. It all begins right there in the *soft palate*, and a simple breath through the mouth will get you started every time. It is important that the breath be consistent, the same way every time. That is one of the technical aspects that you really have to learn and on which you must concentrate. Let me caution you here—we are speaking of *high breath*. I want you to practice breathing in that way only. Later on I will add other elements to *high breath* so you can fortify your position.

While on the subject of *high breath* and *soft palate*, I must introduce you to one of your new terms: the **portal bones**. Don't look up this term in any medical dictionary, because you won't find it there. But my students are very familiar with the *portal bones*, because I made up this name to help explain the pathway for the breath. It's easy to find them by following these directions:

Take a drop of tea tree oil on both thumbs. (Don't ever be without this stuff! You can get it in any health food store—it's a fantastic antiseptic. Use it very sparingly. It sensitizes the area and your feeling will be heightened.) With thumbs pointing upward, trace your top teeth until you reach two round little bones just behind your wisdom teeth. (If you don't have wisdom teeth, don't worry, the *portals* are always easily found.) You must spread your lips to get your thumbs that far back, so your tongue will automatically drop down. By taking a *high breath upward* (past the hard palate, uvula and into the *soft palate*) you will feel the pulling *backward* and *upward* of the *portal bones*, guiding the tissue of the *soft palate* in the right direction—**up** and **back**.

"Now, now..." you may be thinking, "don't tell me that bones move. Bones cannot pull *up* and *back*." You will encounter some concepts here that you may never have perceived before; but if you open yourself to the possibilities, you will notice how easily you will change—not only your perceptions—but your habits, as well. We are able to achieve anything with our minds. If you fathom the movement of the *portal bones upward* and *backward*, it will help you to accommodate the movement of the *soft palate*. This movement is extraordinarily important in our process. By just pulling back on the *soft palate*, you will understand the movement of *high breath* and will have made a very important discovery. Do it often to remain very familiar with this process, and make sure you allow yourself to be aware of this movement at all times. Do it in front of a mirror and see what happens.

The *portal bones* not only serve as guides for *up* and *back*, but also as sentinels for **not** allowing the voice to go below that point. As long as the voice is above the *portals*, you are in a safe zone.

Most of us speak inside the mouth. If you check yourself, you will see that you make the words right around the area of the *portals*. Well, from now on, do not create words in that area. (Remember that for later. It's a little early to go into greater detail, but just understand that the *portal bones* are very important.) The minute the sound/word falls below the *portals*, you will crash into the larynx and the throat. So, may I again suggest that you begin cultivating this movement? The further you are able to stretch the *portals backward* and *upward*, the further back the *soft palate* can go; and that means more height, width, vibration and size of sound.

Now let's recap *high breath* and what should happen if you are doing it right. Three things will automatically occur:

1. Your *soft palate* will lift *upward* and *backward* because you are moving it with air and with the help of the stretching of the *portal bones.* (You can watch the uvula in the back of your mouth rise up. It will almost disappear in the process.)

2. Your tongue and larynx will drop, completely opening your throat (if you have a highly developed Adam's apple, you will see it drop with this process; if you have a smaller one, you will feel the movement of the larynx downward).

3. The air will move downward through the column of air, and your diaphragm will expand.

These three things must be accomplished with the intake of *high breath.* Every time. No exceptions.

This discipline is the beginning. You will be ready to take the next step once you 1) Get used to the idea of breathing through your mouth and feeling the coolness on the *soft palate* and its movement *backward* and *upward* and 2) Know how to "move" your *portal bones* and have experienced the *drop* of the larynx and the tongue.

Now you know how to open the throat and feel the air rushing down the column of air to the diaphragm.

[A note of caution here: **Do not breathe through the nose.** Forget that the nose exists. Concentrate only on developing the sensation of breathing through your mouth and remember, guide the breath *upward... high breath*. Never lead the air *downward* into the throat. If you lead *up*, the voice will begin *on the top*. If you lead down into the throat, that's where you will start. So be very conscious of always feeling for the sensation *on the top*. We will get into more details about the nose a little later in the book].

Think of all the air in the diaphragm. What goes down, must also come up again, so by slowly pulling **inward** on the pelvic muscles (which hold up the diaphragm and are located all the way on the bottom of your belly), the air is once again moved up, in exactly the same way it came down. The throat must be kept *open*, the larynx and tongue *down* and the *soft palate up*.

Essentially, what you must understand is that the voice is air; and the more air you give it, the more beautiful the voice will be. Taking this premise into consideration, the building up of air, the strengthening of the pelvic muscles and the flexibility of the muscular movement of the diaphragm are all tremendously important. The more air you can get into the diaphragm, the more there is to move.

The deeper the air in the diaphragm, the higher the *soft palate.* **Remember, *depth* is *height.*** Think of every breath as though it were the last one you'll ever take in your life. Imagine your head under water. You have one chance to take in enough air to survive. You get the point. This breath must be deliberate, as everything relating to the quality of the voice depends on it. Please be careful never to make it choppy or shallow. An even breath is the beginning to an even voice.

Now let's look at exactly what the air accomplishes. I'll give you a couple of examples to help you understand. Visualize of a fountain that is thrusting its water up into the air. Picture a ball on top of the water and imagine the ball being carried by the water pressure and kept in place. Then think of the fountain being shut down. What happens? The ball falls immediately. The same holds true with the voice. Drop the pressure of the air from the diaphragm, and the *soft palate* will fall instantly. When that happens, the voice position falls, and you are right back where you started—in the throat; therefore, keeping the voice *on the air* is crucial.

Another analogy: Think of an oil drill digging deep into the ground. Suddenly it hits oil, and the black substance shoots up into the air. If there is nothing to catch it, the oil will simply return to the ground and diffuse. Well, for our purposes, the air is the oil, and the *soft palate* is the receptacle. It's the same principal: the air and the way we move it are basic to the voice. We speak with it, and we live by it; naturally, we must also make it the basis of our singing.

Let's talk about the larynx and *open* throat for a minute.

If there is no air, you will push the voice forward. The larynx will come up and try to help you make the notes and, therefore, close the throat. The sound will be much lower than it should be (you may experience phlegm and scratchiness), and the larynx will vibrate. That is unacceptable. In my opinion, the laryngeal vibrato (vibration created by the movement of the larynx) is a defect in the voice and is the beginning of the end of beautiful singing. Vibration is created naturally by the air and air movement *if* the voice is in the correct position.

Pushing air forward closes the throat, and the air can no longer move up. You can pull *in* on the diaphragm all you want, but the air will not pass through a closed throat. The larynx must be in a *down*, relaxed position at all times; and the throat must remain *open* in order to let the air pass freely and reach its ultimate target—the *soft palate* and the *hole.*

You must be aware that as you are reaching the heights of the *soft palate* you may feel a head rush and get a little dizzy. Not to worry... that is because the air is moving into spaces where it has not been before. Continue to strive for height. It's an indication that you're on the right road and, as the body becomes used to it, the heady sensation will go away.

I promise you, though, that before it goes away, it will get a bit worse. This is because as you are opening higher spaces, the air gets closer to the brain. The closer you get the air to the brain, the dizzier you'll feel; however, with constant use, the brain will get used to the extra oxygen, and the dizziness will stop.

Did you know that the greatest enemy of the voice is the tongue? Well, think of it. Most of us move the tongue backward when we sing. I don't really know why, but we do. It's one of those reflexes that is definitely not in our best interest.

The tongue must be flat and limp at all times. It must lie relaxed in its bed and be used only for pronunciation and annunciation. In other words, the same as it's used when we speak. It must never—I repeat **never,** move to the back or rise. If it does, it will close the throat. Try it, and you'll see what I mean. Make a real effort to keep the tongue flat. **Rest** it against the roots of your lower teeth and keep it there until you need it for making your words, just like in speaking. You might find it difficult at first, but it is essential.

Most of my students consider this a really big problem, because they never paid attention to the tongue. But keeping the tongue still is an absolute necessity in your progress. You might say, "But aren't there some singers who lift the front of the tongue up?—And famous ones at that?" True, but it's unsightly and wrong. *Open throat* must be accomplished; and most singers don't know how to do this, so they use the lifting upward of the tongue as a crutch. Keeping the tongue still and relaxed must be accomplished. Keep it limp, flat and down.

To recap our first steps again:

1. Lead a *high breath* from the mouth all the way into the back *(soft palate, hole).*

2. Lift the *soft palate* with the breath and the help of the *portal bones.* (The *soft palate* is the place all the way in the back, where you feel the coolness of the air.)

3. Drop the tongue and the larynx.

4. Open the throat.

5. Allow the air to move down through the column of air and to reach the diaphragm. The diaphragm expands and pushes out.

6. The pelvic muscles immediately lock up and begin to pull the air *in* and *up,* thus keeping the *soft palate* in a *lifted* and *high* position. The larynx and tongue remain *down,* and the throat is *open* as the air passes through. Always think of leading the air far *back* and *high* up on the *soft palate.* That will cause a pulling back sensation of the throat. Perfect. The further back the better. The more pull you accomplish toward the back, the more ultimate power and depth of the voice you will achieve.

One thing that may help you conceptualize the larynx more easily is that the vocal cords are in a box. There can be little movement inside that box. Remember the violin? In order to tune and play the instrument properly, it had to be taken out of its case and put into its rightful place under the chin. To take the voice out of its box, we begin by placing it on the *soft palate*, which has enormous possibilities. **It can move *up* and *back*, create space for making the sound and enable the air movement.**

The larynx will try to come up and help you, but must be kept *down* under all circumstances. NO MOVEMENT PLEASE. The natural vibrations of the voice have nothing to do with the larynx. When the voice is in the right place, the vibrations will be steady and equal throughout the entire voice. The steadier you can keep the larynx, the easier everything I'm explaining here is going to be for you. Please make a most serious effort here. (If you are singing in the right place, and the larynx come up—you will hear the most awful gargling sound and feel discomfort.)

When a box is closed, nothing can come out of it. There is no exit from the bottom of the throat. In order for the air to do its thing, it must rise to the top. That's where we want it, *on top of the soft palate*. For now, please try it that way. Later we will add other features that will enhance and grow the space we need for the voice.

7. Keep the tongue flat and limp at all times and use it only for pronunciation and articulation (diction/ consonants) of the words, just as you would in speaking.

How to Move the Air

chapter 3

How to Move the Air

We talked about taking a *high breath* through the mouth. Now let's become a little more precise. What exactly does that mean? Think about it. If you move the air down, toward the throat, you will have a problem getting it back up to the *soft palate*. If you move the air to the *soft palate* and feel the coolness each and every time you breathe in, you will always be moving the breath in the correct place.

Open the mouth just slightly as we did before. Concentrate on taking the breath just under your front teeth, right above the tongue. Feel the air moving *backward* and *upward*, passing the hard palate, the uvula and the *portal bones*, and lifting the *soft palate*. This is the natural passage of air; anything else is unnecessary and will not achieve the desired results. When the coolness of the air hits the back of your *soft palate* you are in the right place. We talked about this before.

Now visualize (being able to do this is very important) the air hitting the back of the throat, lifting the *soft palate*, opening the throat, dropping the tongue and the larynx and moving downward into the diaphragm. Then picture the pelvic muscles locking up, pulling the air back up through the air column toward the *soft palate*. All this takes just a second. Now you have two air sources on top of the *soft palate*: 1) air from *high breath* and 2) air from the diaphragm. Both sources converge on the *soft palate* lifting it up to maximum height, opening and exposing the *hole.*

When you look into the mirror and watch yourself taking a *high breath* as we discussed, you will see the *hole.* It seems to be pulling further back as you pull on the *portal bones.* Correct. Try always to have this picture in your mind. It's quite important that you see what is happening there in your mind's eye (the *third eye*).

Put tea tree oil on your thumb and stick it straight back into the *hole* until you feel bone. "Disgusting," you may say... Well, perhaps, but it's part of your body; and you have to be in touch with it in order for it to do what you need. Pull the air slightly *upward,* and your thumb will enter into the *hole,* just beyond the *soft palate*; lift gently. You will feel the upper end of the *hole,* and now you will easily understand into where the air has to move. This is a large space filled with great possibilities and is extremely important in the understanding of voice production.

It is from the *hole* that the air passes into the *giro,* or the *turn of the voice.* We will speak about the *hole* more extensively in Chapter 4. The important thing is that you find the hole and are able to lead the air into it; it is the entry way for the air, creating the bottom of the *giro.* I refer to this as the *"back door"* of the voice.

So, now we have the air in the *hole* all the way in the back. What now? How do we move it? What happens next?

High breath has moved the air toward the *soft palate,* has opened the *hole* and created the bottom of the *giro.* Air will now enter the *giro,* will float *over the top* of the *soft palate,* then turn and exit, creating sound (See drawing, *Air*

Movement). The sound will turn and angle toward the *third eye.* Speech will complete the movement by pulling the sound toward the word at the lips; it is there, and only there, that sound and word come together.

There is only a split second between the raising of the *soft palate,* the turning of the sound and the actual exit of sound and word. We will call this *lagtime.* This is one of the most important actions in all of voice production, but right at this moment, I simply want you to know that it exists. I promise to talk about it more specifically later.

It is the word that moves the sound. The *intention* of the word will take just as much air as it needs in order for sound and word to couple and exit together. This is a very important thing for you to remember: the more forward the *intention* of the word, the *higher* the sound can move inside the *giro*. The word *intention* is crucial here. *Intention* is mental, not physical, so all you have to do is *intend* the word to be *forward,* and it will be. YOUR THOUGHTS PROPEL THE ENTIRE SYSTEM. YOUR BRAIN HAS TO BE IN CHARGE.

Never push the voice! Never push the air *forward.* If you push, you will move air against the larynx and lift the larynx. Make the effort of keeping the air always moving *upward* and *back.* The air, which moves *up* from the diaphragm, keeps the flow of the air to the *soft palate,* **keeping it lifted at all times**. The *soft palate* keeps the *giro* and the sound in position. The more flexibility of the *soft palate* you develop (movement by air), the higher the sound can rise. Speak the words as *forward* as you possibly can. Feel the vibration of the word on your lips. **Do not make the word in the *back*. The *back* is reserved for sound; the word is always made in the front, on the lips.** Only when there is a differentiation *(lagtime)* between the sound position and the word position will the voice be in place.

If you move the word *backward*, you will collide with the flow of air and the sound. This will create too much pressure on the *soft palate,* and the sounds will fall. Result: You will *drop,* and this will cause you to sound as though you swallowed a potato. The drop will simply close the throat, thereby closing off the air supply—and you know what that means in the long run.

The air, therefore, must always be kept in the *back*. You never physically move it. It stays there. Sound and Speech will take as much of it as they need for the production.

Your job is to keep the air steady, making the movements that have to be made (*up* and *back*) on the *soft palate* to accommodate the height of the sounds you need. **Please, absolutely no pushing toward the front**. The more air that remains in the back, the longer your phrases can be, and the more flexibility you have for the movement of the *soft palate*.

Think of a balloon, sitting between the opening of your throat and your *soft palate*. Imagine that the opening of this filled balloon is letting air out only to the top of the *soft palate*. Conserve this air in the back and simply speak in the front. That is your job: to conserve air, to speak and think sound.

Let's stop here and talk about some very important concepts. I know most of you think there is some magic formula to the voice. I hate to disappoint you, but there is not. There are, however, a number of rules which must be observed at all times. This part is not creative. This is technical execution. It must be the same way, every time, consistently. The more mechanical the intake and distribution of air, the more freedom you will have for the interpretation of the music and the lyrics.

And the less you will have to worry about running out of it or having the voice fall. It's like starting a car. You turn the key in the ignition, and it starts; you shift the gear, and it moves; you give it gas, and you're on your way.

Here are some ground rules:

1. **Allow the voice to be natural.** Get out of its way. Let it do its own thing. The voice knows instinctively where it has to go; it really doesn't need your help. All it needs you to do is guide the air and distribute it. It needs you to speak and to support the diaphragm, but that's it. **You cannot make the voice.** The less you do as far as actually manipulating the sound, the better. Count on the brain and its innate knowledge of the instrument. **Be in complete control of all the important functions we are talking about.**

   By the way, have I mentioned to you that you already know everything I'm teaching you here? The information I'm giving you is not new to you; consciously it is, but subconsciously the instrument already knows everything we are discussing here and identifies with it. The instrument was given to you in perfect working order along with the original package of your talents and attributes. I call this *Birth Knowledge*. All you and I are doing here is rediscovering the original blue print. I'm bringing it back to your conscious mind by re-familiarizing you with the original set of instructions, which along the way we seem to have misplaced or forgotten.

2. **If you feel the voice, you are definitely doing something wrong.** The natural voice is free and easy, uninhibited. There is no need to push—ever. Pull the diaphragm a little harder for very high notes, but never

ever push the voice! Allow it to flow from you. Guide it, but do not force it. When you are in perfect position, you will not feel anything. It will seem that it is floating, that you are doing nothing at all. **You will feel vocally out of control**. You will think the voice is somewhere above you—and it is. The feeling is totally liberating. Wait till you discover how utterly fantastic singing can be.

3. **See the voice**. Visualize the spaces, the places, the system. The more in tune you are with your body, the more successful you will be in arriving at your final destination: a beautiful, trouble-free instrument that is tuned to perfection. The sounds are visible if you open yourself up to it. Close your eyes and allow the breath to be your guide. We will discuss more about visualization as we go along.

Until now I have not mentioned a very important part in our quest for the voice: the *third eye*. It sits in the middle of your forehead, between your eyebrows, above the bridge of your nose. It is extremely important, not only when you are actually visualizing sound, but for over-viewing the entire system. If you close your eyes and concentrate, you will find that you can actually see through the *third eye*. Sounds dance before you. You can see the air carrying the sounds to the *soft palate*; you can see the pelvic muscles flexing; you can see the opening of the throat and the dropping of the tongue and larynx resting in their *down* position.

The *third eye* opens up another dimension to the voice. By cultivating its opening, you are not only privy to the secret of the voice, but also to the secrets of the universe. The more you see the sound through the *third eye*, the more you are concentrating on the top portion of your head—and the better your chances of reaching the highest possible position. Try it. I am sure you will open yourself to a whole new way of *touching* the voice.

4. **Do not make the voice.** The voice cannot be constructed. The instrument is already there. All you need to do is tune it. Don't try to be something you are not or make the voice into something it is not. If you are a light lyric voice, don't try to be a dramatic voice. Accept your gift and do the best with it that you can. Use it wisely, because if you don't—the ONE who gave it will take it back, and you will lose it. Allow the brain to take over—neither force nor push are needed; common sense and natural instinct will go a long way. If it feels right, chances are that it is. That does not mean that you should work haphazardly, or without using all the tools you've been given so far. All I am saying is that any kind of strain, feeling cramped or need for pushing is unnatural and should never be part of your vocal training.

I do not know how many singers I have met who have told me that throughout their studies, they knew something was wrong with the way they sang. They felt it… the sixth sense of the singer. Go with it—always!

Listen to your inner voice; it never steers you wrong.

I have taught hundreds of students and not one has ever complained to me about experiencing discomfort of any kind when using these methods. On the contrary, they were amazed at the comfort they felt. I constantly ask. The kind of relationship I have with my students is one of total frankness. We talk about the voice, their feelings and exactly what they are experiencing. I feel very strongly that excellent communication between teacher and student is necessary in order to produce the results we are looking for. I know what I know from experience with my students and from... well, we'll talk about that later.

5. **Do not stretch the voice beyond its limits**. Everyone has his own instrument, and each instrument is as individual as the person in whose body it is housed. How many wonderful voices have been ruined because of straining the voice to the maximum? And why? If you were blessed with a certain sound, why make it into something that it is not meant for?

A tenor, who has a Bellini, Mozart or Donizetti voice, should not sing Massenet, Puccini or Verdi (except early Verdi, perhaps, and similar repertoire of other composers), etc. At least not in the beginning—and especially not if he is very young. An Aria of the opera perhaps, if he or she feels comfortable; but no more than that. In time the voice will grow; it is a natural, muscular process; but that growth should not be motivated by the needs of the opera house, the manager or money. Think of what you are doing. Singing heavy repertoire today means the loss of the instrument tomorrow.

Oh, I know about pressure, the jet-age singer, the demands of the career; but I also know that voices used to last for a life time and that the great singers of the past sang until the day they died—and they sang a great variety of repertoire. The secret being, they never sang "out of their voice." No matter what role or composer they approached, they always sang in the same way, using the instrument in the same manner. No changes, no bellowing or dropping the voice to achieve a darker sound. Natural and free always. Listen to Gigli singing *Nessun Dorma* or to Caruso singing *Una furtiva*.

More sound is not accomplished by pushing *down* on the voice, but by pulling it *up* and *back*. The larger the *giro*, the more depth to the sound.

Many singers of the past would sing beautifully until the day they died. Very few singers today last that long—too few. Careers are short-lived, all because the voices are overtaxed and technically not used properly. If you sing the way we are discussing here, your voice will grow naturally and will serve you a very long time. So please, take care and do not overstep your vocal limits.

6. **Trust in your breath.** It is the lifeline for the voice. It's always there when you need it. Learn to use it to your best advantage and make it work for you. Sounds too simple? Forgive me, but I cannot make it more difficult. That's all there is. Actually, as I said before, you already know everything that I'm telling you. When you received the gift, it came with a set of instructions that you, unfortunately, did not follow from the beginning. Perhaps, you think all this too simplistic. It just couldn't be right. It sounds too easy. I called it *Birth Knowledge*. Don't be upset; today is the beginning of the rest of your life as a singer. If you **really** listen to your body, internal voices and instincts, you will see that they will not lead you astray.

I cannot tell you where specific notes are made. The master computer, "THE BRAIN," only knows where to put them. I can only teach you **where** the places for the sounds are and how technically to get there. The technical things that we are learning now have nothing to do with artistry. This is something that simply has to be learned, abided by and secured. The technical aspects of voice production can be applied to any voice, male or female, high or low. It is simply the way the voice is constructed. The idea that there is a different technique for a tenor voice than for a bass, in my opinion, is absolutely wrong. God did not create different body constructions for different voices. Larger and thicker vocal cords, perhaps, but the parts are all the same; and the place where the voice lives is also *always* the same. The consistency of technical execution is what makes it or breaks it. If you listen to Caruso or Chaliapin you will hear the positioning in the same place. The same ring to the voice, the wonderful height, the depth of sound, the brilliance in tone.

The artistry comes with interpretation, phrasing, musicality, etc.—but not in technique. Great singing simply does not exist without great technique. A synergy must be accomplished in order to achieve perfection in the voice. Trust your instrument and inner senses to know what feels right. Trust your breath to find its natural spot. You know, the Designer thought it all through perfectly and gave it to you intact. So why argue with perfection? Accept it and allow it to happen.

Your hearing is paramount, of course. Its message to the brain is translated into action, and your body will do the rest.

Focus on these three little words:
- **LISTEN**
- **INTERPRET**
- **EXECUTE**

Listen to the sounds. Hear and see the sounds in your *third eye*. Allow the brain to **interpret** the music and find the exact position of any note. **Execute** by *pulling in* on your diaphragm, by allowing the sound to move effortlessly and then by speaking the words. Pronounce properly. **The *intention* of the word is very important,** and diction (pronunciation of the consonants) is crucial.

I cannot emphasize this enough. The more *forward* you are with the word, the greater the potential for keeping the voice in line. **Remember, it is the word that moves the sound, not your pushing and forcing. Sounds are always moving in one direction only: *up* and *back*—**no matter what. **The lowest sound, therefore, is the highest one *up* and *back*.**

Stay in line, moving *upward* toward the tips of your ears on a slight angle. Get away from the idea that the sounds have to be pushed out of your mouth. Pull *backward* and *upward* on each sound, no matter how high or how low. The word is always in the front. Understand that sounds are always moving over the top of each other. **The *giro* moves *up*, never *down*,** so the sounds are carried *upward* in a **spiral-like motion**, attached to one another (*legato*), never dropping. If you can assimilate this concept, the battle is almost won. Go for depth— depth of *high breath* into the *soft palate* and the depth of air into the diaphragm.

chapter 4

Placing the Sound

Now you have taken the right breath. Your *soft palate* is *up*, your tongue and larynx are *down* and the throat is *open*. The diaphragm is extended; the pelvic muscles have locked up; and you are pulling in to get the air back up—all the while keeping the throat *open*, the tongue and larynx *down* and the *soft palate up*. Now place the first sound right *on top of the soft palate*. Let's backtrack again to find our way.

Put some tea tree oil on your thumb and follow me exactly: Start at the front teeth (on the inside of the mouth) and move the thumb back along the hard palate. You will feel a hard ridge between the soft part and the hard part. Pass the ridge and move your thumb all the way to the back. Feel your uvula (the little thing hanging that has no apparent purpose), go past and push up gently. You will feel the *hole*. **Keep pushing up with your thumb to familiarize yourself with it.** It's terribly important that you know precisely where it is. Then take a breath, the way I explained before, and immediately you will feel that the *soft palate* moves up. Yes, now you've got it. Keep your thumb there and do it again.

In the beginning, this might cause a gagging effect in some of you; but in time, and as you get more familiar with the feeling, this reflex will stop. For now, suffice it to say that the *hole* plays an incredibly important role in our work, and the more you can get "into it," the better it will be for you.

The most important thing you must remember is that the *soft palate* moves, but it needs air to do so. As long as you keep a steady flow of air and you keep the diaphragm pulling in to get the air up, your *soft palate* will move to make all the notes you need.

It's vital that you remember that the *soft palate* must move *up* toward the top of your head. Let me rephrase that. Imagine your *soft palate* moving *up* towards your *third eye,* while simultaneously pulling toward the back of your head. The higher you move the *soft palate* in the *up* direction, the more flexibility of the voice you will have. The further you move it toward the *back* of your head, the wider and rounder the voice will be. **The voice moves from the *top* (of the *soft palate)* to the *top* (of the *third eye*), and the further you move the *soft palate backward* (with the help of the portals), the larger the space you create. THERE IS NO DOWN POSITION!! Everything that you have to do gets done right there, *on the top*, above your *portal bones*.** Everything depends on the understanding that the voice moves *from the top to the top*.

If you move *down*, your voice will fall into the abyss of the throat. If you start in the throat and try to move *up,* you will have a break in the voice—and that's ugly. Stay up there and feel what happens. All of a sudden you'll have an incredible height in the voice—no more falling and cracking, no sudden register changes that make the voice sound different on the top, in the middle range or on the bottom. Total ease, no strain; and all because of this one little place. What a revelation! Try it.

Remember the rules we talked about? Here are some more to add to the list:

1. **Never pull on the voice.** Allow the air to do the job. The air will not hurt you, force will. In other words, don't look to make the sounds from the throat—no manipulation of any kind, please. Simply float them on the air *on the top* and leave them there. There is no need for pushing and forcing. Get out of the way, mentally and physically. Allow the sound to happen naturally and watch the voice respond with ease. The power comes from the air, not by pulling and straining.

2. **Try to keep your mouth as small as possible.** Pulling the jaw down will pull *down* the *soft palate*. All the work you are doing to keep it up will be in vain if you rip your mouth open. **Remember that singing is speaking.** How far does your mouth open when you speak? Please keep this in mind. It's vital. If you open too much, the precious air will escape much too quickly, and you will not have enough to finish the phrase.

   I know this is contrary to what most students of the voice have previously learned; but try it yourself, and you will see. Of course, there are times that you must open a bit wider, but always be moderate and remember: not too much. Think of a reversed megaphone, small in the front and wide in the back.

3. **All notes are made in the same place.** High notes, low notes, all notes. And all voices. There is no need to switch your position. The top is your comfort zone. Always. Without exception.

   In order to achieve a homogenized sound—top to bottom, even and harmonious—you must remain in one position. You can color the voice any way you want, but in the same spot. You will never sound like you have two, or even three, voices—just one beautiful sound throughout the whole range of your voice.

Think of a violin. From the lowest notes to the highest, its sound is even, beautiful and in line. If you listen to the greatest singers of the past, such as Gigli, Bjorling, Caruso, Wunderlich, Pons, Chaliapin, Curci, Pinza, Fagstadt, Ponsel, Tebaldi, Bastianini, Melba, Scipa (and even those who were not considered the greatest, but had only medium-sized careers), you will hear that their voices were placed in one position. They stayed in that place and did everything seemingly effortlessly. No straining, no scratching, no flat or sharp notes. Just gorgeous, floating sound, all in one place. That is the way the voice was taught at that time. Somewhere along the way, something changed. The voice became secondary to the career.

4. **Float all sounds on the air.** Think of every note as needing its own air in order to exist. *Without air it fails; with air it lives.* Our bodies need air to survive; so do the sounds we make. Concentrate on producing as much air as at all possible and use it sparingly. Keep all the air in the back. Don't let it go by pushing it forward. Speech will take as much air as it needs. There is no need to make an effort to push it forward. If you do, you will most likely disturb the larynx—and you know what that means. Air moves all by itself. Remember what we talked about before? The balloon filled with air?

5. **Emphasize your words.** If you do not place the words all the way in the front on your lips, you will obstruct the flow of air. I cannot stress enough that the sound and

the word are made in two separate places: sound on top of the *soft palate* and the word with the teeth, lips and tongue. You should feel a slight vibration of the words right under your nose on your lips. The more to the front you are in your diction, the more you will free the *back* and the *top* to do their thing. If you concentrate on the *word,* the *high breath* will find its natural place and do what it has to. So concentrate on your speech; it's imperative. Think of almost spitting out the words— not screaming, but really over-pronouncing them.

6. **Let your two front teeth be your guide** and use the tip of your tongue; use your lips, but keep all movement to a minimum (just as in speaking normally). The less you move the mouth, the more stable the position. The **impostation** of the word in the front is directly responsible for freeing up the opening on the top. Very soon, when we add the final element to this puzzle, you will understand this point even more so.

7. **Smile in the *back* by lifting the *portal bones*. Put your smile *into your eyes*** and see what happens. Stand in front of a mirror and watch yourself. Imagine that you can only communicate with your eyes and that you wish to tell someone you love them, but only with your eyes. Feel your *soft palate* rise, almost automatically. Feel your cheekbones rise. **Keep that smile in your eyes forever.** You will not fall nearly as easily because the voice is in a high position and in a much safer space. Believe it; it works like a charm. Don't smile with your mouth until after you finish singing; and always keep the front teeth delicately covered. Pulling the lips apart spreads the sound; it squares off the back, and that you do not want. Our intention is to

keep the entire mouth cavity as round as possible. A square peg does not fit into a round hole; and if you think of the entire system, everything is round: the *hole*, the *soft palate*, the opening to the throat, the column of air, the *giro*—all round.

Your face muscles and your jaw should be fully relaxed, as should be your chin and mouth. All the vowel sounds are made *behind your eyes.* **Actually accustom yourself to speaking *behind your eyes*; that is, form your words *behind the eyes*.** You've never thought about the fact that the eyes speak, have you? Amazing. Well, it's high time you do, because with our work you'll find that this concept will make the whole conversation come together and will keep you *high* at all times. Have patience... soon you will understand clearly.

chapter 5

The Giro: What is it?

The *giro* (also called the *turn,* or the *endless loop)* is one of the most important features of the voice. When you can feel it and conceptualize it, you will understand why the voice stays in one position and how it is possible to make all sounds without switching to different places. All the notes that you ever want to make are made inside the *turn of the voice.* Round and round, forever *turning.* I hinted at it when I told you that the voice moves *up* toward the *third eye,* and when I mentioned that pulling the air *back,* thereby creating a larger space, will allow the voice to widen and grow larger. This *up*-and-*back* movement of the *soft palate* facilitates the creation of the *giro.*

When you listen to great singers, you will hear that they make transitions with great ease; they're inaudible, totally in line. The voice just went to where it had to go… even, beautifully, without difficulty. They were turning the voice. They were using the *giro.*

Of course you remember the *portal bones* and the *hole,* which we talked about before. You also know by now to smile in the back and to put your smile into your eyes. You are also aware that by taking a *high breath,* the *soft palate* and the uvula will rise and create the space needed to open the *giro.* And you know that the throat has to be *open* and the tongue and larynx have to be *down*. So basically, all is set for the *giro* to *turn* the voice.

Now we are going to get a little more abstract in our thinking and feeling. All the way in the back where the throat ends (where your thumb could not go further because you felt a bone) there lies the secret of the *giro*... the secret of the voice, the secret of life itself: **The *bone of life*! The *bone of life* is the beginning of the *giro*, the springboard, the lowest part of the *giro*, the depth of each individual note.** Don't look for this term in the medical dictionary, either. Like the *portal bones*, it is an expression and image I use to help you understand where we are going.

Kabbalah, the ancient mysticism of the Torah (Judaism), explains that the *bone of life* [which lies exactly between the bottom of your cranium and your first vertebra (atlas)], contains all the DNA necessary to recreate a human being. It is said that on the day when the Messiah comes, all those *bones of life,* which are the **only remains** that don't turn to dust throughout the millennia, will once again be used as the basis for human forms and will again be the receptacles for souls.

I have thought about this a great deal, and now I understand that the secret of the voice lies exactly in the same place. Find the place in the back of your head (it's almost like a little indentation) just in between the cranium and the first vertebra and familiarize yourself with it. Find the same spot internally (by taking the breath to the furthest point in the back of your throat), and you will have unlocked the mystery of the voice.

If you pull the air all the way into the *bone of life* (keeping the air placed there as much as you can without pushing it *forward*) and from there shoot it *up* into the *giro*, you will achieve perfectly placed sounds; this combines the bottom, middle and top of each individual note—homogenized sounds that don't break registers.

All registers (I object to that terminology, but use it because you are probably familiar with it) are contained inside the *giro*. All sounds, all colors, aperto/coperto, ciaro/scuro—all of these depend upon the movement of the *giro*. *Light* sounds are further to the front and the top of the *giro*; *dark* sounds are further back and toward the depths of the *giro*; *open* sounds are more to the front; *closed* sounds are further to the back. But they are all inside the same *endless loop*. No switches of position are necessary to achieve an incredible diversity of sound, yet all are positioned in the same place.

Sound too easy to do? Is it too hard to believe? Too far out? Perhaps, yet in my studies with my students, I have found time and time again that this concept has opened the door for them to understand the *giro* perfectly. So I suggest that you give this a chance without prejudging. Let yourself experience the power of the *bone of life* and with it, the full opening of the *giro*.

So, here we are: air pulled back by the *portal bones* to the *bone of life*, the *hole* opening and the air moving up and back towards the *third eye*. This is your point of entrance, and from there you do everything you have to. You will notice that in this position, you'll have maximum capability of movement, and the voice will feel easy, round and high. This is the way to get you into the final position. Perfect this movement and very soon, we will add the last fragment of our puzzle. Have patience; you're doing great. Again, you might feel a little dizzy, and that's a good thing. Please remember this place for further reference as we go along.

The light-headedness comes from the air. You are now able to move very high and can continue climbing. Think of your whole head opening up, without a cap, to accommodate the air. Are you surprised at the height you can achieve? Well, don't be. Everything is possible with the *giro*. **It *turns* the sounds *over the top*,** through the *third eye* and then sends them to the teeth and lips to couple with the word and exit together.

What you will begin to feel now is wonderful resonance in the entire mask and head. The voice will ring *high, round* and be perfectly in position. The vibrations of the voice will be perfect. By the way, if you feel the sound ringing in your ears, you are a little too low. Pull the air further *back* and higher *up*, and the sounds will move up causing the ring in your ears to go away.

Think of the *giro* as a Ferris wheel. Round and round it goes. All the cars are attached to it and they, too, are going around. Imagine car #5. Get in it. The motor begins to move, and your car is climbing higher and higher through various positions. But car #5 always remains car #5. Well, that is the *giro*. It takes the notes, on the air, into the stratosphere— effortlessly. All sounds are made in the *giro*. One great turn is capable of creating every sound you will ever need.

If you drop outside the *giro*, you'll be on top of the larynx, and you know what that means. Keep the air *high* at all times in order to move the *giro*. Keep the air from the diaphragm coming; it supports the *giro*. Remember that the motor (diaphragm) must never stop. Keep the smile *in your eyes*.

This is your safety zone. Nothing can happen to you there. Stay there and bask in glorious sound. Perfect this position, and you will never have problems. Only there can you be truly comfortable. Only there lies the real beauty and total freedom of the voice… its roundness, depth and height. Technically, this must be perfect every time. **This is one of the major keys.** This begins to open the door to the voice; this combined with all the things we have yet to talk about will allow you to be vocally liberated.

So now you know about the breath, the diaphragm, the *soft palate*, the *giro* and the way to move the air from the top of the *giro* to make the word. You see how easy it really is.

This analogy might make it easier to visualize: Think about a bow and an arrow. Think of pulling the bow string all the way back, tightly, until you cannot stretch anymore. Now release. The bow will fly in the direction to which you pointed and hit its mark (depending of course, upon how good of a marksman you are). If you guided the arrow low, it will hit low. If you aimed high, that's where it will go. The great marksman hits the center every time, because he is exact in his technique. That is what is required of you, and the way you aim the breath will determine whether you reach the *hole* and the *bone of life* and go into the *giro,* or not. Make this your top priority.

If you take the air full and high through your mouth, the air will move deeply into the *bone of life* and the *hole* and create a powerful *giro*. The deeper the penetration of the air, the higher the *soft palate* will be; consequently, the higher the sound. The further *back* you pull the *soft palate on the top*, the larger and rounder the sounds will be. If you concentrate on that, you will notice that the air will go into the right place every time without your even thinking about it.

The whole procedure becomes instinctive and, after all, that is what we want. You do not have time to think about these things when you're singing. You have to worry about music, lyrics, stage directions, your partners, etc. The last thing you will want to think about is where to put the voice and how to do it. You'll be too involved with other things. It will take a little time for the brain to understand this, but believe me, it will.

Think of a baby. When it is born it can hardly do anything; but as it grows, it learns all kinds of responses. First turning, then crawling, then sitting, then standing and walking. All that takes time. The brain has to adjust the body to all the new information. The same holds true with what we are doing.

For so many years you have done it in one way. Now it is time to change. New information must be assimilated, and the brain will do so; but your job is to train it to think that way by itself. **You must develop the thinking process. Always think, "*up* and *back.*"** The full, total sound of the voice begins *on the top* of the *giro*, in the *third eye* and ends on the *top*, in the *third eye*. That is essential. Begin with the smile in the back. This movement of the breath, as we are learning it, must become automatic and reflexive.

I think at this point you are sophisticated enough to understand the *giro*. Now it's time to put all the parts of the *giro* together. Here is the final movement which has to be achieved in order to produce a complete, 360 degree turn that begins at the *soft palate,* the *hole* and the *bone of life* and finishes at the front teeth and lips with the coupling and exiting of sound and word; it then pulls *backward* and *upward* and starts all over again. Each sound is made that way. Each sound has its own individual mini-*giro*. (Coloratura has micro-*giros* that turn extremely fast). No matter what you wish to do, and **no matter what your voice,** the *giro* is where it lives and thrives and grows.

The final step in creating the totally integrated *giro* is the NOSE!

Remember in the beginning, I asked you to not breathe with your nose? I wanted you to learn how to move the *soft palate* and to understand the *bone of life*, the *portal bones*, their movement, the *hole* and, of course, the beginning of the *giro*.

Now, however, it is time that you **allow** the air from the nose to **simultaneously** rise with the air from *high breath*. Don't pull the air through the nose, simply think *up* and *back*, and the breath will carry the air through your nostrils to where it has to go in order to open the chamber.

Think of smelling a rose; it's no more than that. Make believe you are in a meadow and dew fills the air. Flare your nostrils slightly and move air through the nasal passage, *upward*. (If you are having trouble doing that, take two *q-tips*, and slide them up your nostrils very, very gently. Then pull both of them outward and allow the breath to go through the open space. You will feel a real coolness from the air, and it is that kind of feeling that you want to recreate every time you breathe).

The bridge of the nose becomes immensely important in creating the highest opening to which we can lead the air. **This is the front door of the voice; the back door is made up of the *portal bones*, the *hole,* the *soft palate* and the *bone of life*.** When you are allowing the air to lift *up*, through the nose to the bridge, imagine two big flaps opening outward and allowing the air to flow through. The air then diffuses under the eyes, just above the cheekbones, moves back, lifts the *soft palate* to its highest position and allows for the full opening of the *chamber*. **Now the entire space for the *giro* is created.**

Feel that. Do it over and over. Those flaps in the bridge of the nose must remain open at all times. That is essential. Air rises, not only when you take the breath *up*, but always. **So by keeping this passageway open at all times, you are getting a constant supply of air.** This air supports the top of the *giro* (the *third eye*), where you need to be. So make sure never to push the air into the nose; but always, as you have learned to do with mouth air, move toward the *up* and *back* position—toward the tips of your ears, deep into the temples.

As the *chamber* opens, you will feel the top of the *soft palate* rising to its maximum position. When you feel this opening and are dizzier than you have ever been, you know you are in the final place of the voice.

It is in there that the movement of the sound actually takes place. That is where the *giro* lives. You will feel a lifting sensation at the *portal bones* pulling *up* and *back*, a further rising of the *soft palate* inside the mouth, the dropping of the tongue and the larynx, the *opening* of the throat and movement of air *down* the column into the diaphragm. Everything—the entire system—now functions as a whole. That lift of the air through the nose completes the space for the entire position for the voice.

Do this slowly and smoothly at first, then more swiftly as you become more proficient. Notice that the air moves *up* and *back behind your eyes*. **Feel** the actual movement of the air. Become very familiar with this place. **It's the final number in the equation.**

If you do this very naturally, you will feel the complete opening on the top, almost like a secret room opening up to accommodate the breath. **There, and only there, is the true final place for moving the voice.** In this location is the culmination point of all sounds. It is here that the 360-degree turn occurs; this is the home of the *giro*. This is where it all comes together—where it all happens. This is the place of movement of the voice. This is your safe zone. **Only by breathing simultaneously from the nose and mouth (in the way with which we are now quite familiar) can you achieve the absolute control of the sound. Every time!**

The consistency of taking the breath is really what this is all about. Doing it the same way every time; not thinking about it at all, just allowing it to be completely instinctive; trusting that the brain, which recognizes this spot as the true home of the voice, will know precisely where every note goes—without your interfering. **You can really do nothing physically in this place.** Here the **thought** and the **air** rule. The more freedom you give your thoughts to actually process the sound, the better and more precise the sounds will be.

The *giro* is by far, and without any doubt, the great secret of the voice. Please read this chapter repeatedly and train your brain to think of the voice in that way. I promise you incredible results.

Now lets talk about *lagtime* (See drawing, *Lagtime*). *Lagtime* is the time it takes air from the **nose** to do the following:

- Lift to the top of the *giro.*
- Lift the *soft palate* to its maximum height.
- Open the *chamber* to accommodate the whole movement of the *giro.*
- Create all the sounds inside the *giro (*the *endless loop).*
- Turn the sounds toward the *third eye.*
- Bring the sounds to the front teeth to couple with the word (diction) and exit together.

The sounds remain in the *back*, are turned *over the top*, lead to the word and exit together. In this action, there is a split-second interval for the *turning* of the *giro.* Without *lagtime*, the voice will not stay on *top.* Instead, the sounds and words will mingle in the back and fall. With *lagtime,* however, the sounds are free to be *turned* by the *giro* and brought toward the word.

When you take a breath simultaneously from the mouth and the nose, the air from both areas comes together, turns *over the top* and moves toward the *third eye.* **There you must**

think of beginning and ending the voice. It's your highest point of reference and the perfect angle for sound and word to couple and exit.

Please, practice this often. The millisecond it takes for the *giro* to turn and for the word to bring the sound to the front in order to exit is of the utmost importance. The more you concentrate on speaking the words in the *front*, the easier this will come to you. Remember that without observing *lagtime*, word and sound will begin in the *back,* and the voice will fall.

In that split-second, all the sounds are created by the brain. Your only job at this point is to do the following:

- Allow the sounds to move *backward* and *upward* into the open space (you are always moving toward the open space behind your eyes, toward the temples, toward the tips of your ears).
- *Intend* the word as frontal as possible.
- Support the *soft palate* with your diaphragm, which in turn supports the *giro*.

Let this happen all by itself. **Your "thinking" is more important than your "doing."** Allow flow on the top, and you will feel the kind of freedom about which I spoke previously.

chapter 6

Spinging: the primal scream of the voice

Another new term I'd like to introduce you to is *spinging*. (and like some of the others, you won't find this word in the dictionary). It is a methodology that I developed for and with my students. I have no idea if anyone else is using something similar, but I have found *spinging* to be vital in training the brain to understand the *giro*. *Spinging* is a combination of speaking and singing. Since they are, as I mentioned before, the same, you should have absolutely no problem doing this.

Imagine speaking in one place and singing in another. The switch is difficult, so why change at all. Allow the singing and speaking voice to be in the same place, and you have solved a major problem.

We know that the voice has to be on the *top*, in the *third eye*, on *top* of the *giro*. Let's review how to get there and then learn how to *sping*.

1. **Allow** the simultaneous breath (mouth and nose) to flow upward. (The key here is **allow**.) Make believe you are smelling a rose and feel the coolness of the air lift your cheekbones, the *portal bones* and the top of the *giro* into the *third eye*. Always keep the smile in the eyes. This entire motion opens the chamber behind your eyes to accommodate the turning of the sound.

2. Follow the breath as far back and high up as it will go, and then (using *lagtime*) make a sound—turning the *giro* and saying the vowel sound "EE." You will find that you can almost feel the air moving into the **spheres of your eyes.** When you are aware of this, you will find the voice very easily—because it is there that the *giro* is made and the voice can achieve true freedom.

3. Pull the breath further *up* and further *back*, while creating a loop that turns the sound round and round behind your eyes; always turning over the top, say, "EE,EE,EE,EE,EE,EE," pulling the air *up* and *back* with the muscles behind your eyeballs, etc., until you have no more breath. Always end the sound on the *top of the giro,* never the *bottom.* In this way, you will achieve a small, vibrant sound that you can only make very large by pulling *back further* and *higher* and giving more air. The more you get into the head with the sound, the better. Remember to stop the breath on the *top of the giro*, in the *third eye.* You will feel a pulling sensation. **That tension must never be lost.** If you lose it, the *giro* will drop the sounds.

   Take another breath and start all over again, all the while pulling the *portal bones* and the *soft palate* further *back* and higher *up.* You will feel incredible vibrations resonating throughout your head, in your eyes and in your mask. Your ears might ring. The feeling is almost indescribable; but once you have it, you will never let it go. Those are the vibrations of a healthy voice—not the *vibrato* of the larynx. Imagine that you are actually pulling sound through the nose, depositing it all the way in the back of the chamber, turning it over the *top of the giro* into the *third eye,* round and round. In the beginning *sping* softly, and as you become more familiar, add diaphragm (more air) to the *sping*.

You will notice that the more you *sping*, the larger and wider the sounds will become. You are spiraling *backward* and *upward* toward the tips of your ears and past them toward the *bone of life*, which completes the total ring of the voice. The further back you go, the larger the voice gets. The deeper into the *giro* you move the *sping,* the greater its potential for **coloring** the voice.

It's time to choose a piece of music. Breathe simultaneously, the way we now know. Keeping the melody in mind, begin *spinging* it in "ᴇᴇ," exactly as though you were singing it. Find the absolute highest spot (usually an octave higher will do just fine). That should put you right into the *top of your giro*. You will hear the voice very, very high and buzzing in your head. When that happens, you know it's right.

Do not sing, rather *sping* in the maximum height of the voice, *behind your eyes,* on the *top of the giro*, in the *third eye*. **Imagine the sounds moving into your head, one by one. Make each *giro* wider than it needs to be.** Really pull on the *portal bones* and the *soft palate*, higher and higher—as far back toward the *bone of life* as you possibly can. Please remember that **the only way into the *sping* is through the nose breath**. The nose breath will bring you to the *top of the giro* every time. But caution: *Do not involve the throat in any way under any circumstances!!* You must not feel any pulling or tension in the throat. It is imperative that the larynx remain in *down* position and the throat remain totally *open*, with the tongue relaxed and low in its bed. Begin *spinging* gently and increase in volume as you become more confident and more familiar. The *soft palate* must be in *high* position; and the facial muscles must be relaxed, as should be the mouth, the tongue, etc. **You are moving sound in the chamber behind your eyes (in the *giro*) and with your eyes ONLY.** Never allow the diaphragm to relax. It is forever pumping the air up in support of the movement of the *giro*.

After doing this a number of times, the melody will almost naturally come into the *sping*, because essentially, that is what you are doing—you are speak-singing. I ask you to please remember that even in *spinging*, like in singing, the sounds move *up* and follow each other, **one sound turning over the *top* of the other.** The voice becomes larger and louder and goes higher and higher until you feel at ease with the piece you are *spinging*.

Now, begin vocalizing the whole piece in "EE." Simply sing the melody in "EE" and remain entirely in *spinging* position. You will notice how easily even the hardest notes will come to you. After you have done that, attach the words and sing the piece. Believe me, I have done this with my students thousands of times. Pieces that initially seemed impossible became easy and sat in the voice like a glove. ***Spinging* is an essential way of putting a new piece of music into the voice. Don't worry about sounding like a fire engine. With every *sping* you are building the position and the size of your voice.**

You will also become aware that your speaking voice will change in the process. It will be higher and will have more resonance to it. It is not that your timbre will change, or that from a Bass you will suddenly become a Tenor; but you will notice a wonderful height and ring to the voice that you never had before. The more you *sping*, the more the voice will sit in its rightful place. The wider you *sping* toward the back, the larger your voice will get; and the more depth you will achieve. It's a wonderful tool. Use it to put your repertoire into the voice. You will be truly amazed by the results.

The concept of *spinging* is incredibly valuable because you can really get in touch with what *high* position is really like. After a while, this will become natural and necessary for you. You will automatically go into the *spinging* position when you begin singing, and that will give you the height and ring of the voice that so many singers lack today.

If you do not like to *sping*, if it's hard for you or if you don't like the sound you make while spinging, I must tell you that it will take you much longer to understand and grow the voice without *spinging*. I have had students that have refused to *sping* because they thought it silly or unnecessary. Well, I certainly cannot make anyone do what he doesn't want to; but from the experience I have had, and from the successes of those who have *spung* religiously—I strongly suggest that you give *spinging* a real chance to guide your voice and to grow it.

Listen to the greatest voices, and you will hear the *sping* in the sound (squillo), the ease, the flow, the utter height and freedom. Please do this and do this often—especially before tackling new pieces and certainly with those that have been put into the voice long ago, but aren't yet comfortable.

chapter 7

The Art of Humming
and its Importance

We have talked about quite a number of things that I am quite sure are new to you and that you have never heard before. That's what this is all about—opening yourself up to the voice and all its possibilities. "What," you may ask, "could be new about humming? I know how to hum." Well, I'm sure you do, but perhaps I can add something new to your humming experience.

1. Close you mouth and take a breath through the nose **only** (you know how to do that by now—not by pulling the air *up*, but by **allowing** the air to flow *upward* and in a very relaxed manner).

2. At the *top* of the breath, all the way in the back where you feel cool, *drop* the first sound, *turn* it and hum at the lips. Don't forget that even in humming, just like in *spinging* and singing, *lagtime* is essential. Do this a number of times, and you will find that the voice automatically goes into the right place and easily makes mini-*giros* without any effort whatsoever. You are floating sounds into the head. Think of the sound entirely *behind your eyes* and turn the hum around the *giro*, in the *spheres of your eyes*. As I mentioned before, the sound is made in the *back,* and the word (diction/

consonants) in the *front*; so don't forget that even in humming, the same principal applies. Always keep the point of the word at the mouth; otherwise the sound will fall.

3. The more you hum in that way, the higher the voice will go and the deeper toward the *bone of life* you will move. That is precisely what we want to achieve. If it's wrong, you will feel the involvement of the throat, crackling or tightness. You'll feel the uvula moving, the *soft palate* dropping and the larynx will come *up*. When it's right, you'll feel a heady sensation, perfect vibrations and clear, beautiful sounds.

4. Now, open your mouth slightly. Take your simultaneous breath using your mouth and nose in the same position as when you were humming. Make the sound, turn it and speak the vowel. That is the perfect way of setting the voice. You will notice that the humming and *spinging* positions are the same. Humming just produces a smaller sound. Everything that we are doing is designed for one purpose only: to put the sound *high* and keep it there. All that we've done, from the very beginning of our journey until now, works together in harmony.

5. The further *back* you hum, the easier the height will come. The more you concentrate on reaching the *bone of life* and pulling your sounds *up* and *back*, the greater ease you will achieve. Hum often; it will help you familiarize yourself with the spot, and you will ease into it without any difficulty… instinctively.

6. If you have trouble finding the position, take a nose breath and immediately close your nose with your thumb and index finger. Hold it closed and place the sound *above the bridge of the nose, behind the eyes*. Keeping

the nose closed in such a way shows you exactly where the sounds are rotating and whether you are pushing the sounds into the nose, which is an absolute no-no.

Remember that we are training the brain to recognize the natural position of the voice so that you can be as free as possible to concentrate on the music, the words, the conductor, etc. Let the brain do its thing; it is so adept at what it should do. It knows exactly where to go and what to do, so get out of the way, and let nature take over.

In the journey we are on to find the natural voice and in everything that we have discussed so far, we are essentially trying to achieve an alignment of conscious and subconscious knowledge.

Let me explain that a little more clearly. The subconscious knows all the information. The conscious knows only the information that it has lived by for so long. At this point, I am introducing data attempting to substitute new ideas for old ones. This is the alignment I am talking about. When the conscious mind knows and understands what the subconscious already knows to be true, you will have achieved alignment. That's what it takes. **Once this is done, a physical and mental balance is achieved, and the voice will remain in its natural place and grow comfortably.**

A note of caution at this point: the conscious mind always wants to go back to that with which it is familiar. The old way will always creep in, and doubts will always appear—especially when you are not yet sure of what you are doing. You will find yourself many times wanting to chuck it all and do what used to be uncomfortable but sounded better, bigger and meatier.

That is a natural reaction, a human one. But I implore you— for the sake of your voice—be patient. Give the *giro* a chance to grow, to develop the depth you need in the voice. The more space you open, the more you will be able to move into depth, hence the greater the power of the voice. It takes a year for most (a bit more for others) to develop that kind of dexterity within the *giro;* it all depends on the instrument and your allowing the process to take place. Don't expect that just by opening up the space, it will immediately give you all of the voice at once. The movement must be cultivated, worked on, opened and freed. Let nature do what it needs to do, and you do what you need to do. **If you do not develop the diaphragm along with the *giro*, the voice will remain much smaller and will have a tendency to fall.** If the diaphragm is powerful, and the *giro* is developed, the voice will stay in perfect position.

I say it again and again—please be patient and work on all the principals outlined here together in order to achieve the desired final result: a voice that is resonating, is vibrating in perfect harmonic pitch, has its position secure and is beautiful to listen to.

chapter 8

The Jaw

The jaw is a great enemy of the voice—not quite like the tongue—but in another way. I am always amazed when I watch singers. They rip open their mouths to such a degree that their tonsils are practically visible. It's unsightly, but more importantly, it is prohibitive to everything we are trying to accomplish with the voice.

Think about this, or better yet, do it. Pull the jaw down and feel what happens. There is tension on the chin and on the muscles of the throat. Everything we are talking about here has to do with being as natural as possible, remaining stress free and keeping the sound *up* and in place. If you're pulling down on the jaw, you are pulling on the height of the *soft palate* and achieving exactly the opposite of that for which we're striving.

When you are speaking, how much of the jaw are you using? Practically none. The natural drop of the jaw is all you need, so what sense could there be in ripping the mouth wide open when you're singing? I know this goes against what others may say, or perhaps what you see many singers doing—but think about this: The voice begins *on the top* and ends *on the top*. Keeping the voice in line *on the top* is what we are trying to achieve. Completely opening the mouth would directly influence the smooth movement of the sound and the air *on the top* and pull it out of line. Another thing to consider: the larger the opening, the more air escapes. Obviously, that is not what we want. On the contrary, we want to preserve as much air as is possible in order to move the *giro*. So, the smaller the mouth in emission, the more air is conserved and the more precise your diction.

Of course there are times when you need to open wider, but there is never a need to overdo it. The jaw, just like the rest of the muscles in your face, should be relaxed. There should be no pressure of any kind anywhere (other than the diaphragm, of course). Give yourself to the music, the lyrics, the action on stage. The Italians call it "*faccia stupida*," a dumb face: there is no muscular action (total relaxation produces beautifully even sounds); no pulling on the mouth, just speak; pulling the air only behind the eyes. The more you do this, the easier the air moves into the head. Remember please, sounds are moved only *on the top*, *behind your eyes*. The air from the mouth moves from the *top* to the *bottom* and to the *top* again, but sounds must remain *turning* only in the *giro*. Any muscular movement on the *bottom* (throat, larynx or tongue) will affect the flow of the air and, therefore, the sound of your voice. In order to have a beautifully homogenized sound, allow the air to move freely and interfere as little as possible.

Concentrate on your speech *behind the eyes* and the **formulation of the vowel sound *behind the eyes***—inside the *chamber*, where the voice lives. The more you accomplish this, the less you will feel the need to pull on the jaw.

Let's talk about the actual *word* for a moment. **Pronunciation, articulation (diction/consonants)** and **intention** are imperative to the *word*. As I have already explained, you do not have to pull on the jaw to articulate and pronounce properly; just the opposite is true. If you keep the mouth in a normal position, as in speaking, the tongue, lips and teeth will have a much easier time producing what you want. Also consider this (better yet, feel it): when you pull on the jaw, your whole facial physiology drops, and that is definitely contrary to all our desires. So please remember to not strain or pull on the jaw. The *word* is natural, easy, loose and entirely without strain, yet at the same time it is intentioned and powerful.

Keeping the jaw un-pressured will also allow you to keep the *soft palate* from falling. If you pull down on the jaw, you are losing air; and since by moving the jaw down, you are also pulling the soft *palate* down, you have to work so much harder to keep *high* position.

So, what good can come from opening too wide? None. You are only making your job more difficult and working against yourself. In order to keep everything *round* inside, you must maintain the jaw in its natural position. When I recap everything at the end of the book, I'll talk about that again; but in the meantime, just remember that you need no more action than is required in speaking. It's as simple as that.

Visualization

chapter 9

Visualization

From my explanation of the previous topics, I am certain that by now you understand many of these new concepts. Paramount to this process is *visualization*. We mentioned it earlier, but now I want you to really concentrate on it. In working with my students, I have found that the more they are able to come in contact with their inner-selves, and the more spiritually they are *attached*, the easier they comprehend the concepts I have explained.

I spoke about the *third eye* and opening it. Believe me, once you discover how to make use of it, the *third eye* will be of immeasurable help to you. By focusing the entire voice into the *third eye* you ensure that your thought processes will always be *upward;* and since the position of the voice is *up*, that's just the place where you need to be. With a little practice you develop the ability to see the entire movement happening. You'll cut out all the extraneous ideas about the voice and put only the things we have talked about here into your mind. You will see how easily your brain will adapt to this very basic way of perceiving the voice.

I could give you all kinds of medical terminologies, but that is not the purpose here. I want to talk to everyone who wants to speak better and sing beautifully. I believe that everyone can; and although a great deal depends on the instrument you were given, there is no reason for speaking incorrectly. Guttural sounds are not necessary, and with a little effort and a shift in your thinking, we'll change all that.

I have developed this entire concept with great care. I do not want you to be confused in any way. I want this to be easy. Oh, I know you are going to be frustrated at times. That's quite normal. But I promise you that if you persevere and do what we are discussing here, within a fairly short period of time (I would say four to six months) you will have most everything under control and will feel fantastic vocally. Trust yourself, your own system and your own motivation—you will be happier with your voice than ever before. Just don't give up and think that you're not progressing fast enough. It takes a baby a year to walk, two years to talk and three to be potty trained. It took you all your life to get to a point vocally that you know is not good for you and where you are not achieving the desired results. So take the time to experience and explore, and you will see the rewards in the beautiful impostation of your instrument.

Envision the voice exiting through your *third eye*. Don't think of it as coming out of the mouth. If you do, you are already too low and too close to the throat. Keep your mind set on *height,* and you will have it. Think about it constantly. The more you do, the more intimate you will become with your instrument— and that is precisely what is needed.

You must know the voice in order to use it properly and to not damage it in any way. So please, take the time and make the effort to open yourself up and use the power of the *third eye.* You will be surprised how much it will help you tune your instrument and accomplish what you want—not only with the voice, but in your life.

Listen to your instincts. Listen to the inner voices in your body. They will not steer you wrong. **It has to *feel* right**. If you experience any type of discomfort, chances are you're on the wrong track. Let your body guide you. As I said before, you already know all of this; it came along with the gift. Allow it to flow from you. Try not to interfere.

Remember that you cannot *make* the voice. All you can do is be its guide, and the guide has to know where he is going and what he is hoping to accomplish. Set your goal and do it right. Follow what I have taught you, and the voice will not fail you. Just give it the time it needs. PATIENCE, PATIENCE, PATIENCE.

Let me spend a moment giving you some of my thoughts on the brain as it applies to our work here. The more you allow the brain to take over what you are doing, the better. The more integrated you are in *right* and *left brain* activity, the easier it will be for you. Creative? Or logical? Most of you probably think of people as being one or the other. Well, in singing, speaking and communicating, we have to be both—especially in voice production. In singing, we must allow the brain to take over. It's difficult for most of us, since we have been trained to manipulate the voice from early childhood. Because of this training, most of us became even greater experts in *making the voice*. Now I am telling you to let go completely; to stop controlling; to learn to trust the natural instincts of the brain; to be a guide, but not to manipulate. And it's true. The more you let go, the better it will get. But you must know what your job is:

- **Breathe correctly.**
- **Speak.**
- **Support properly.**

Think about speaking. Try to imagine having to find every word somewhere in the brain. Where would you begin looking? You have no idea, and neither do I. We can only be the guides who lead the breath into the right place and allow the brain to take over from there—just like it does when we speak. Instantaneously. If you *think* it, you can *speak* it. Well, if you *hear* the sound, you can *sing* it. When you are in the right position *(behind your eyes, high up and back)*, the brain produces all the sounds in the *giro;* and you do no more than hear the sounds in your *third eye*, speak and support.

That is the ideal position of the voice; and that is what you should strive for, whether in your speaking or your singing. The brain will compute sounds instantly once it knows the information and understands it. Reread these chapters many times to fully comprehend what I'm saying. When you do, the brain accepts this information and it will become an instinctive response; thus you are free to do what you need to. The brain knows the way so well. It recognizes the place from the original blueprint (*Birth Knowledge*) and responds instantly. The voice feels so much at home in this territory.

My students are always amazed at how when they let go, they feel nothing. That can be very perplexing. After all, we "must" be in control, or so we've always thought. Well, here the control lies in knowing what you are doing, and the better you are at **feeling**, the better the voice will respond. Don't worry, in reality you're still in charge. You're simply allowing the brain to take over at what it does best. Let go and trust the natural wonder of creation. Besides, you have plenty of other things to think about!

Phrenology is an ancient science dating back as far as the Atlantean Era that predicts human behavior through the precise calculation of various skull measurements. Well, just a few days before actually finishing this book, I took some days off to concentrate on the last editing changes and went to see friends in Daytona Beach, Florida. Their home is filled with collectibles of strange and beautiful things. In my room, I noticed a bust with outlines on the skull. I picked it up, and upon closer examination, was simply amazed at what I found.

I immediately realized from the drawings that there was a correlation between my work with the voice and Phrenology. While studying the drawings, I realized that where we are placing *language* and *vowel sounds* (eyes) is the precise place Phrenology places verbal memory and verbal expression. Then I went to the back of the head, into the *bone of life* area, (the focal point of the entire movement of mouth air to the back) and found that that place is associated with the love of parents, of children and of animals; in other words, the most profound of human emotions. Then I moved to the *third eye*, the place where we begin and end the voice and the drawing caption reads, "individuality, mental and physical." Of course this makes total sense in our work: the mental work done by the brain and the physical breath combine to create the individuality of the voice—speaking, singing and communication as a whole. Then I searched the top of the head, and the precise spot where we are centering the voice is interpreted as, "spirituality, hope, faith and wonder." The area of the temple is described as, "tune and modulation" and is exactly where we are placing the movement of the voice inside the *giro*.

Can you imagine how profound this experience was for me? I wrote these lines to include them in the book and to make you aware of this science. There is much information available on the Internet, for example, **www.phrenology.com**. There are also books on the subject; but I believe that for our purposes, the information I've just shared with you confirms that the path we are taking is the correct one.

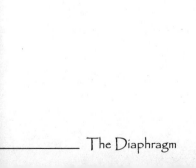
The Diaphragm

chapter 10

The Diaphragm

The diaphragm is the motor, the support system. Using the diaphragm is really not complicated, but it is of the utmost importance when it comes to using the voice correctly. Think of a beautiful car without a motor, or a gas tank without gas. That is the relationship of the diaphragm to the air. The air is the fuel that makes the motor run, and a full tank gives you freedom to take a long drive without worrying. Fill it up to the brim and go. The more you have, the less you need to pay attention to the mileage—right? Take this thought and transfer it to the voice.

We know how vital air is to the voice and that every note needs its own air on which to float. If you have no air, you have a problem. It is up to you to provide the air by breathing properly and making sure that the diaphragm is full and that the air is distributed properly. I always tell my students that the diaphragm is the support system to *high breath* and to the *giro*. **It does not make up for *high breath***, but it **supports** *high breath* and, therefore, the *soft palate*. If you breathe into the throat and then use the diaphragm to support the voice, you will still remain in the throat. If, however, you use *high, simultaneous* breath to get into the *soft palate* (the *hole,* the *bone of life,* the *giro*) and start *on the top* (*third eye*), the air from the diaphragm will support the height. The diaphragm, as I have mentioned before, should grow in size and power as the *giro* and the voice develop. If the diaphragm does not grow , the air will fall; and the sounds will not grow properly or develop the depth needed. I cannot over emphasize how important the use of diaphragm is; so please, from the outset of your work, do not slack off on exercising the muscles that are needed to support the diaphragm. Coordinating the movement is not easy and takes concentration as well as physical effort; but you must achieve the balance needed in order to maintain the height of the *soft palate* and, therefore, the total opening of the throat.

Use the diaphragm in three instances:
1. On the attack of the first note.
2. On the high note.
3. On the last note (**absolutely essential**).

Why? If you do not have enough air for the first note, the *soft palate* will not go into maximum position, and your start will be low. For the high note, or the highest note (and the lowest one for that matter), the *soft palate* has to move further *up* and *back* to create more space. (Low notes need as much diaphragm support as high notes; please keep that in mind at all times. The *soft palate* must remain lifted for both low notes and for high ones.) The air will supply the necessary power to do that. And on the last note, the diaphragm must be used because high air is running out; we do not want the *soft palate* to drop and the note to wind up low, crashing into the throat. On these three occasions, you should make a concentrated effort to pull on your pelvic muscles in order to lift the air.

This is a guideline, not a rule. Use the diaphragm in these three cases; but preferably, at **all times**, continually. It is best and safest to use the diaphragm with every note. That way you know you're supporting each sound; and you guarantee that at the end, you'll have plenty to **finish** *on the air* and not *in the throat.* Controlling the diaphragm's power is a challenge to which you must pay close attention.

The more muscular reflexes you develop, the better. The diaphragm is a tremendously necessary asset to your voice. It's your air storage tank. You can count on it to help you out. It's like a life jacket for the voice. It helps you float your sounds. Remember to pull on the diaphragm gently but consistently. If you pull too hard, the palate will shoot up too high, and you will be sharp; if you don't pull hard enough, you will be flat.

Another case I've observed with many students is that if you pull on the diaphragm too sharply, the air comes up too fast causing the larynx to rise; the tongue also pushes up, and thus, closes the throat. If you are pulling too hard on the air, the larynx will mistakenly get a wrong impulse. So be careful. Learn how to control diaphragmatic power. The air from the diaphragm must be led to the **back** of the throat, pass the larynx unnoticed and go straight to the back to the **soft palate** in order to do the job there. If you lead the air to the front of the larynx, they will come *up* and will prevent the air from hitting the *soft palate;* it will get stuck in the throat. **All air, therefore, is led to the** *back*—**to the** *soft palate,* **to the** *hole* **and** *into* **the** *giro*—**as close to the** *bone of life* **as you can possibly get.**

If you only count on the diaphragm for air, you will have the tendency to not use *simultaneous breath.* You will lead the air into the throat, and that is a big mistake. Please be aware of that. **The diaphragm is a vital support to the** *high breath* **and the** *height* **of the** *soft palate.* The first step is attaining *high breath*, and the next step is maintaining it. That is the job of the diaphragm.

Keep the diaphragm working at all times. Do not let it drop.

If you let go of it, the air in the air column will also drop; and that makes the *soft palate* and the sound drop, which in turn cause the larynx to rise. The larynx want to help you out in making the note, but will ultimately close the throat instead. **The diaphragm helps the sound begin and end *on top of the giro* in the *third eye* and supports it in that position.** The last note is completely suspended on air, and the air is closed off *on the top* in the *third eye.*

This is what it looks like: (See drawing, *Last Note*).

The diaphragm is pulled in tightly, all the way, and held there. The air column is holding the *giro* and *soft palate* in the *up* position. The last note, therefore, is supported by the air column and the *giro.* The air is cut off right on the top, in the *third eye.* Remember that the voice begins and ends in the *third eye*—not by lifting the tongue and not by closing the throat; simply by shutting off the air *on the top*, just like closing a faucet. If this is done incorrectly, you will hear an ugly, choppy sound at the end of the phrase; and we don't want that.

Think of it this way: the note is on *top* of the *soft palate* in the *giro.* The sound remains suspended on top, the throat remains *open* and the larynx and tongue are *down.* The *high air* and the *intention* of the word *turn* and carry the last sound to the front teeth where it mingles with diction and ends. No chopping, no fallen notes—just a note suspended on air, floating.

Now you can see how important this motor is and how much depends on your being able to master its use.

Exercise is very important in developing the pelvic muscles. Here is one that you should begin immediately. Lie on the floor, legs stretched out. Slowly lift both legs together, all the way up. At the same time breathe in. Your diaphragm will extend.

Hold it there. Then slowly move the legs down and allow the breath to float out gently. Do not tighten the throat while you breathe in or out. The only things that are tight are the muscles that support the diaphragm. Do about 25 of these every day and watch how much power this will give you in just a few weeks. As with all exercises, the beginning will be a little painful; but it will be worth it in the end.

As those muscles get stronger and stronger you will be able to control them at will. Your brain will accept this information gladly and use this support system with pleasure, so much so that it becomes instinctive. After a while, you won't even think about it anymore. Because this is such a crucial aspect of using your voice correctly, spend some time in cultivating this most important support system.

Troubleshooting

chapter 11

Troubleshooting

I need you to be hypercritical with yourself now. Always work with a good tape recorder. Keep all of your tapes, and don't erase them. They will serve you later when you need to check something specific. Listen and re-listen to your voice, and if you hear the slightest imperfection, do it again. Before you try again, though, you must know why the sounds were not good, why the voice cracked, why it went sharp or flat and/ or why you ran out of breath. You need to listen, *really* listen, to your voice. Every sound counts. Every feeling is important.

Now I want to help you along in shifting your thought patterns by sharing some of the most common trouble spots I have encountered with my students.

1. The voice is too low or not on pitch.

This happens all the time, and the reason for it is very basic. You are not starting the voice *on the top of the giro*, in the *third eye*. If you start low, you cannot achieve *height*. If you do not pull the *soft palate* to its maximum position from the beginning, it will be very difficult to move it *up*. *High, simultaneous breath* plus the attack from the diaphragm will allow you to start the first sound in the correct place every time, and thus, continue the voice in proper position. Remember to start *in the giro* and follow the line *upward* and *backward*. Keep the sound there. Always *high* and always *on the top*. All sounds move *up* and *back*; so the lowest sound is actually in the highest position and the furthest back.

2. The voice cracks.

Obviously this is not permissible. Here are some reasons why it happens:

   a. The elevation of the larynx and the closing of the throat cut off the air.
   b. The tongue is not flat, but instead high in the back, thus cutting off the airflow.
   c. The *soft palate* falls because it is not supported properly.
   d. The voice is not high enough in position; because of improper breath, the voice tumbles into the throat and cracks.
   e. The voice is **pushed** into a place where it does not belong—namely, the throat.
   f. You begin *inside the giro*, lose the support and fall into the throat.

3. The sounds are flat or sharp.

Easy! You're not *high* enough in the *giro;* and if the *soft palate* is not in correct position, the sounds will not be correct. Too high is sharp, too low is flat. Remember that you cannot make the sound, you can only guide it into the right place. The brain knows where the sound you are trying to make goes. It's difficult to accept not being in control, but that's it. Allow your hearing to notify the brain, and let the brain do its job. Use proper support of the diaphragm. Be instinctive. Why do you have to control something that is already perfect? Let it happen. Assist by doing what is asked of you. Breathe properly, support properly and speak *in the front* with teeth, lips and tongue That's already enough to think about. Leave the "making" to the expert—the brain.

4. Potato sound.

You know exactly how to get rid of that. Get the voice out of the throat. Start the sound *on the top* of the *giro* in the *third eye* and *on top* of the *soft palate*. What you are doing is making sound and word in the back, in the same place. That's a no-no! **The word is in the front (diction/ consonants), and the sound is in the back**. All sounds must be allowed to travel *up* and *back* while the words (diction/consonants) stay in the front. Keep the *chamber* **open** at all times and always think of sound, as well as vowel sounds, *behind your eyes.*

Think of speaking the words *behind your eyes* and sing *into the head.* Speak. Speak. Speak. I cannot emphasize that enough. When you place the word too far back, you collide with the sound, and your voice will become thick and throaty. Remember that it's the word that pulls the sound *over the top* of the *giro* and brings it to the *front.* Keep the voice *up* at all times, and the potato will go away.

5. The voice is uneven.

This is more difficult to fix because it takes serious self-critiquing and a determination on your part to achieve an even sound throughout the entire voice. Most singers simply are in love with their own sound. Emotion and passion take over. It is very difficult to remain objective about ones instrument, but please—try to do so. If you can be objective about your own voice, you will find that you will achieve a great deal more. If you allow your passion to take over, you'll never be truly honest with yourself—and that is a mistake.

Notice, by the way, that I never speak about **registers**. I do not subscribe to that belief in the least. **The voice is ONE, from the top to the bottom. There should be no change, no break. No *passagio*!** All notes should be in one position (*on top of* the *soft palate*, in the *giro*) and should flow from there. There's no need for different voices or changes in position.

Resonance's can be found in every cavity of the body, but the only space where the voice is totally comfortable and at home is *on top of* the *soft palate* and in the *giro*—**actually in the empty chamber and spheres *behind your eyes*. The more you lead the sounds into the head, the more resonating and large the voice will become.** If you feel as though the sounds are *beyond your head—outside your head*—then you are correct. The feeling is liberating and absolutely beyond description. At first it may frighten you because you are seemingly out of control, in unfamiliar territory; but ultimately you will know that you have mastered the voice.

One of my students is a very prominent eye surgeon. In our first lesson we talked about what actually can be found *behind the eyes*. In his explanation to me, he referred to spheres. Well, I promptly advised him to place the sounds *behind the eyes* and rotate them around the spheres. In five minutes he understood the concept of the *giro,* and thus, found the true position of the voice.

Not having to worry about different places to put the voice makes it easy on you and the voice. I am not talking about a change in color, *ciaro/scuro*, light and dark. I am not talking about open or closed vowels. What I am saying is that the voice must be homogenized from the *top* to the *bottom*, that sounds can only be even when they are placed in one position and when each note has its own air on which to float. The *top* (the *chamber*) is always *open*; it never closes. The air needs a passageway for the sound in order to be able to carry it *up* and *back* and to turn it over. If you close the *top*, you crush the sound. Only minuscule movement of the lips makes the vowel formation, with no more effort than actual speaking requires. Only rarely will you need to open the mouth wide—a *bit* wider, yes; but only in moderation.

Let us not forget the *intention* of the word. Not pushing the word toward the front, but the *intention*. Pushing is physical; **intention is mental**. If you *think* it, you can *achieve* it. So make your brain work for you. Work smart, not hard!

Also remember that the air from the diaphragm must be pulled in evenly. You must learn how to do that. If you pull sporadically you will be able to hear it in the voice. Every movement, be it in the throat or in the diaphragm, is audible. So forget the throat and learn to move the diaphragm effortlessly. It's a tall order, but you can do it. Persevere, and it will become second nature in no time.

6. Nasal sound.

A terrible habit. It completely takes the ring out of the voice. It happens when the tongue is too *high* up in the back and closes off the passage of air to the *hole,* preventing the *soft palate* from rising properly. The little bit of air that does come up is pushed against the roof of your mouth instead of being able to move backward into the *hole.* Instead of opening the mask, filling it with air and creating powerful resonance's throughout the chambers, the air goes into the nose and creates nasal sound, which is constricted and sounds terrible.

You can feel that easily by taking a *high, simultaneous breath* and then closing your nose with your fingers. Feel the movement of the air. Begin your first sound where you feel the cool spot *on top of the giro* in the *third eye* and simply stay there to continue all the other sounds. (*Spinging* that way is also excellent practice.) You will find that you're in the back on top of your nose. Yes, that's correct—*behind your eyes.* The sounds will simply flow from you.

Keeping your nose closed (with your fingers only—in all other cases the nose and nasal passages must remain totally open, as we discussed) will automatically lead you into the right place. Repeat that many times, and you will get used to guiding the breath directly into the *top*, allowing it to *rise* into the *giro* so you can start there. Keep the air as far back as you can (in the area of the *bone of life*). Remember the balloon and don't push forward. By doing this, you will never have to worry about nasal sounds.

chapter 12

An Overview

The Whole Thing in a Nutshell...
10 Easy Steps

1. Take a *high breath* with the nose and the mouth **simultaneously**. Start at the front teeth, allowing the air to move back (past the hard palate, the uvula and into the *soft palate)* into the hole and finally into the *bone of life*. Feel the *pulling* back sensation of the entire area.

2. At the same time, pull *up & back* on the *portal bones* to lift the *soft palate* and open the *hole*. Allow *high breath* to create the *bottom* of the *giro*, thus opening the back door of the voice. Use the *bone of life* as a spring board and guide the breath *upward* and *backward* at all times. All sounds are formed in the back, and all words are formed at the teeth and lips, using the tongue.

   The *high breath* from the mouth *opens* the throat, *drops* the tongue and the larynx and moves *down* the column of air into the diaphragm, extending it. Keep the tongue flat, limp and relaxed at all times and tucked behind the roots of your bottom teeth. Use it exactly as you would in speaking to pronounce and articulate the word (diction).

3. With the diaphragm now extended, the pelvic muscles immediately lock up and slowly pull the air back *up*, through the *open* throat, the *dropped* larynx and the lowered tongue. Make sure that the air from the diaphragm is even, as any unevenness will cause the voice to be out of line. **On the last note, remember to always cut the air *on the top of the giro*.** Never *drop* the diaphragm before you finish the phrase. If you do, the *soft palate* will fall, the larynx will rise and the whole elaborate contraption we have built will collapse.

4. **Always** lead the air to the back. The further away you are from the larynx, the better; and the further *back* the air stays, the better. **All sounds move *upward* and *backward*; there is no *down* position. The lowest sound is the furthest *back* and the highest *up*. Never push the air *forward*. Never!** Move the air as far *back* into the *bone of life* as you can and use the back of the throat as a springboard to reach the *top of the giro* in the *third eye*. The further *back* you pull the throat, the larger and deeper the sounds will be.

5. The air from the nose couples with the air from *high breath* (the mouth), forms the top part of the *giro*, opens the chamber and begins the voice in the *third eye*. All sounds and vowel sounds stay *behind your eyes* at all times. Nothing is *lower* than the *portal bones*—not the word, not the sound. You must remain above them. The voice begins there *on top of the air* and ends there by your deliberately cutting off the air at the end of the

phrase on the last note. Think of the space *behind your eyes* as actually making the word sounds and each sound moving further *to the top* and the *into the back* of your head. Actually begin speaking inside the *spheres of your eyes* and creating the word there. Speak *behind your eyes* and formulate the words (diction/consonants) at the lips. Little action is required of the mouth; **behind your eyes is where the major work is done**. If you remember to keep the *smile in the eyes* at all times, and if you think of wanting to communicate with someone through your eyes, then you will achieve the proper use of the voice.

6. **All sounds turn *over the top***; nothing from the *bottom*, not ever—not the word, not the sound. Everything comes out of the *top* of the mouth at the front teeth. **Remember that it is the word that moves (*turns*) the sound. The more frontal the position of the word, the more freedom of movement you will have in the *giro*. The front opens the back and the top. Never close the back and never close the top! Keep the space you have created with the nose breath *behind your eyes* open at all times. If you need to cover sounds, do so by pulling the *giro* very wide in the back, turning it as high as possible and closing the vowels with the movement of the lips. That kind of sound will remain *on the top* and will be brilliant, never sounding guttural.**

7. **Observe *lagtime*** (the length of time it takes the air from the nose to form the entire *giro* and all the sounds in it). The *giro* turns 360 degrees from the *back* where it forms the sounds *over the top*, and thus, moves the sounds toward the *third eye* on a forward angle toward the lips. This causes the mingling of sound and word in

perfect harmony. *Lagtime* **is the single-most important movement in keeping the voice** *on top* **at all times.** *Lagtime* **separates sounds from words.** Without it, word and sound will start in the back, and you will either fall into the throat or have the potato sound. The angle of *third eye* and the lips is vital. Stand in front of a mirror and guide the sound from the *back* to the *third eye* with your hand over the top of the head. You will note the angle necessary to have sound and word meet about 2 inches outside your head is just at the level of the front teeth, or more precisely, 2 inches from the tip of your nose. That is the actual coming together of word and sound.

8. Use the diaphragm as a **support** system, not **the** system. It's available for you to use to support the height of the voice and the *giro*. Pull in on the first note, the highest/lowest note and the last note—and at all times in between. Learn to measure the air you expend so you will have enough to complete the phrase (that's what "putting something into the voice" really means.) To position the sound, to position the word and to determine how much air it will take to create the line of the phrase is very important. Pull the diaphragm on the last note because if you don't have enough air, that note will drop into the throat, make a choppy sound and pull the sound out of line. Chances are, the next phrase will also begin there.

9. *Never* sing a piece of music right-off-the-bat. *Sping* it, "ᴇᴇ" it in melody, and then **only** when you are comfortable with the *giro's* placement and the sound should you attach the words to it. *Sping high* and *wide.* The *wider* and *higher* you *sping*, the more depth and height you will acquire; hence, the larger the sound.

Make sure you do not ever touch the throat while *spinging*. Vocalize much, always in *spinging* position. Reread the chapter of *spinging* many times; it's tremendously important.

10. **The diaphragm must grow along with the voice.** Please exercise the pelvic muscles regularly so that when you need them, they'll be ready for you. The voice will grow in its natural position, but if the diaphragm does not grow along with it, the voice will fall. Let me caution you: do not rely on the diaphragm instead of *high, simultaneous breath*. **The breath is essential, while the diaphragm is *support* only.** There are singers who do not use the diaphragm very much, but since they are masters of *high breath & giro movement*—they are able to do incredible things. Please keep that in mind. Most of us mortals need the support the diaphragm provides, so keep doing your exercises. No slacking off; it's dangerous!

chapter 13

The Spoon/
The Egg

At this time I wish to introduce you to your new best friend: the spoon. Using it will help you move the air into the right place. All my students have their own spoons. It's my present to them when they first begin their lessons. After a couple of lessons, they learn to use it; they carry it with them at all times. It represents a special energy to them and always keeps them in the correct position.

Get yourself a *demi tasse* or expresso spoon. They're just the right size. To begin with, place it on top of your tongue, as far back as is comfortable. Now press down gently, just enough so you can feel the spoon on top of your tongue and so that you can feel what happens. Now take a *high, simultaneous breath*. I bet this is the first time that you have felt *open throat*. The larynx automatically drop, and the air moves through the air column into the diaphragm. Can you believe how much air is going down there? That is what you have to get used to, so use the spoon all the time to feel your *open throat*.

Now, the second position of the spoon is on top. Place it directly into the middle of your hard palate (roof of your mouth). You'll notice that the tip of the spoon will hit exactly where the hard palate forms a ridge to make way for the *soft palate*. Take a *high breath* and allow that breath to follow the curve of the spoon directly into your *soft palate*. Then gently move the spoon into the *up* direction and follow with the air. That will teach you the movement of the *soft palate* and help you find the *hole* every time. This, too, will soon become second nature. The little spoon is your big helper. Use it all the time, gently and without force of any kind. It will become invaluable. Carry it with you always and especially before a performance.

The third position of the spoon is really the decisive one. Take the spoon with the downside *up*. While looking in a mirror, put the spoon so far back that it touches the uvula. This will give you a sensation in the end of the throat. Be careful. The round, smooth part of the spoon is lying on top of your tongue, right? Now take in a *high, simultaneous breath*, *open* the throat, *drop* the tongue and larynx and attach a sound with the diaphragm. You have no choice—you must start above the spoon, *behind your eyes*, *inside the giro...* and that is exactly where you need to be.

At first you will gag—there's no question about that; but don't be upset or discouraged by this. Once, twice, three times—every time you do it, it gets easier. And after a while you'll automatically start in the right place—on top of the *giro*, *behind your eyes*, in the *third eye*. Be patient, please. And like the old saying goes, "If at first you don't succeed, try, try again." The means justifies the end. It may sound corny, but it's true.

It may very well be that positions *one* and *two* are enough for you, but if you still find that your larynx are coming up, that you're not opening your throat or that your tongue is still too high in the back, use the **third** position. This is the most difficult way, designed for the true-blue throat singer. Be hard on yourself; I promise that it's worth it.

I cannot emphasize enough that the spoon is your helper. I don't want you to depress the tongue or hurt yourself in any way. Remember to be gentle. This exercise is simply designed to make you feel the sensations of the air more powerfully and make sure that you guide the breath into the correct position. Some of you may think that the spoon is superfluous and not necessary, that you can do it on your own. Well, perhaps you can. My very strong suggestion is to work with the spoon (a metal one only; if you use plastic, there is no transfer of energy). If you use your finger to keep the *soft palate up* or the tongue down, the same principal applies. But if you use a small metal spoon, a foreign object on your skin, you will see how the body responds to it. The effect is quite different and will cause you to make the important and necessary changes in the height of the *soft palate*, as well as the *dropping* of the tongue that will cause the opening of the throat. Learning this will make a major difference in your voice.

I must share something else with you that I only very recently discovered: the **EGG**... yes, the egg. It is the perfect and absolute solution for finally eliminating the most serious of problems: *closed* throat, the *lifting* of the larynx and the lifting of the tongue. I had one such problem with one of my students. The spoon did not alleviate the problem because 1) the student did not like to use the spoon and 2) because the spoon still allows you the opportunity to skirt the issue of keeping the entire mouth cavity open. So I *asked* for help, and the answer came.

For those of you who have a real problem keeping the *soft plate up*, or for those that have a tendency to speak below the *portal bones* (teeth clinchers), this method will make absolutely sure that you have no other place to go—except the right one.

Hard-boil a medium or large egg (depending upon the size of your mouth). Once it has cooled, remove the skin and place it into your mouth. The egg must be big enough to fill most of the space in your mouth but still feel comfortable. Now take a breath through the nose (the way we learned) and place the sound all the way in the *back* (where you feel cool). *Turn* it (*lagtime*), and bring it back to the front. Actually try to form the vowel sounds *behind your eyes*, and you will see that it's entirely possible to achieve that. The *higher* into the *giro* you set the vowel, the better and clearer it will sound. The voice automatically goes into the right place, because you cannot move the tongue (or the larynx for that matter). The throat remains completely *open*, and that is what we want to accomplish. This may sound drastic; but believe me, it works like a charm and makes a huge difference in your approach to *high* position. Keeping your facial muscles very relaxed and close your lips around the egg. Allow the voice into *spinging* position, *at the top, behind your eyes,* **in the giro, inside the chamber.** You will soon discover how simple this is.

All of my students, bar none, with whom I have needed to use the egg, have found the correct place within minutes. Interestingly, because of the position of the egg so far into the back of the mouth, each student began to understand the pulling back of the throat into the *bone of life*. After he took the egg out of his mouth and recreated the feeling of the egg's presence without it actually being there, the voice improved tremendously in depth and volume. Of course, this makes sense. The air from the diaphragm is now able to travel fully into the spaces and is not obstructed by anything—not the larynx, not the tongue. This is truly open throat the way you need it.

As with everything we talk about, care is advised. But don't give up trying. The benefits are certainly worth the effort.

chapter 14

Who & What are You?

Well, by now you know something about the voice, so let's talk about you—you the singer, the communicator, the person. You are different, you know? Very different from others. It's true that a singer is born, not made. The same holds true with the voice—you either have it or you don't (I mean the kind of instrument required to be a singer). A person who is a singer is primarily that—a singer.

I have met many "would-be" singers that were really talented, but in the end it didn't work out for them—not because of the instrument—but because of who they were as people and how they viewed themselves. You cannot be an architect and a singer, or a restaurateur and a singer. It simply does not work. At one point or another you will have to make a life decision: It's either—or. You can sing and own a restaurant and sing in the restaurant, but you will never be a real, honest-to-goodness singer!

There are a million things you can do in your life at which you can excel while doing them simultaneously—but singing is not one of them. Singing is different. Your soul, your passion and your spirit are undeniably connected to your voice. Being a singer is as much of an attitude as it is a vocation.

If you're a real singer, you'll do anything to get to sing. You'll sell pencils in the street (I have met such a person), you'll be a waitress or you'll go to night school and hold a day job just to pay for your lessons. Basically whatever it takes, you'll do it. The voice moves you. It holds you, captivates you, inspires and depresses you. In other words, the voice rules you.

The voice is also connected directly to the heart, therefore, you cannot be totally ruthless, cold and insensitive and also be a great singer. I know this is a lot to swallow, but I'll explain.

I have been involved in all phases of the music business, from teaching, to management, to CD production, to directing and producing. I have met hundreds of singers and taught many, many more. I've been professionally involved with many and befriended most. The outside world plays cruel tricks on the artistic personality. One person has to please so many people in order to make a career. Everyone wants a piece of you, the artist. Sometimes you might see yourself only as a slab of meat in the eyes of those who are looking to exploit your talents.

Remember, as you think, so you are. You and only you are in control of how others see you. If you allow yourself to be taken advantage of, do what others want and do not go by your own feelings and sentiments, you have only yourself to blame. No one can make you do anything. You always have the last word.

Basically, deep down inside (forgetting the outside influences), the heart of an artist is pure. A great singer feels only good when his voice responds, and if he has a bad day—"all the tea in china" isn't going to make him feel better about himself. If the voice does not respond, he feels let down, depressed, unworthy, frustrated. You know what I mean. And there is no cure for that. That's the heart, the passion—this incredible connection between the psyche, the spirit and the voice. When I hear a voice, I melt inside. I turn to mush. I want to touch it and love it. I want to make it the best it can possibly be.

I feel its power and beauty inside of me. I think and dream about it. I imagine how it would sound singing "this" or "that" repertoire. These are powerful emotions for someone who does not sing. But that is what the voice stimulates in someone who listens with the heart and soul. I can well imagine how all encompassing it must be for the person in whose body this voice is actually housed.

How can a vessel containing such beauty be anything but good? Pretty idealistic, huh? Definitely. But that is the voice. The voice is ideal, ethereal, godly. It is beyond human comprehension and will not be denied. If you are a born singer, the voice insists on being heard. Sooner or later you must give in.

I have had some students who are way past the age of sixty, their voices young and unscathed. I have taught them because I understood their need and their passion. In most cases, their lives took on new meaning—they felt rejuvenated and full of life. Their accomplishment was valuable in how it affected their outlook on the future, and I derived great satisfaction in facilitating such major life breakthroughs for them.

If you are having trouble with the voice, I believe there is something wrong with the connection to your heart. Something about the way you view the voice and your life. For instance, if you consider the voice your own personal property, if you think it will perform for you no matter what you do to it and no matter how you live your life—well, think again.

In the beginning I spoke about the voice as being a gift, and so it is. The One who gave it can also take it away. In order for you to establish this spiritual connection that I am talking about, you must dedicate the voice, every day anew. You must have a deep understanding within every fiber of your being that you are the voice, and the voice is you. You must realize that you are a chosen vessel to disseminate beauty and love through your voice.

You are inseparably connected to each other and, without a doubt, influence each other. If your heart leaps with joy, your voice will be soaring. If you are unhappy and negative about something in your life, you won't be able to raise the voice. Have you ever experienced that? I thought so. Take this thought into consideration before you sing and understand that your emotions and feelings play a major role in the way you will express yourself vocally.

There are times in everyone's life in which you have to separate yourself from your voice. By that, I mean that your life as a basic human and your life as a singer cannot always be connected. For example, if you had a fight with your boyfriend and have to sing that evening, you'd better forget the fight. Completely disconnect and just be the singer. Only then will the voice serve you. Easier said than done, but that's what it takes.

People may think you are a miserable person, that you'll walk over dead bodies to get where you are going (oh, the reputations of singers—I know them all too well; and most of what you hear has an element of truth to it—but that's show business!). But when it comes to the instrument you must be a pussycat. You are its slave. It controls your actions and feelings and never allows you to forget who is boss. You must learn to live your life according to the needs of the voice. And your instrument is demanding; you can't deny its needs. If you do, sooner or later it will fail you. So please, be aware.

I explained this to one of my students just today. She partied and drank and carried on until some ungodly hour of the morning and then came to her lesson. Need I say more? The voice needs rest. It needs to be kept sheltered and warm, nurtured. It's within you, so what you do to or for yourself, is going to be reflected in your instrument. Remember that the next time you stay out until all hours and have to sing the next day. Think of the voice before you make decisions of how to spend your time.

> [A sidenote: When you sing the way you were taught throughout these pages, you can sing almost always. If you have a sore throat, a cold or even laryngitis, you can still sing because you are not using **the throat** or **the larynx**. Very, very rarely will you be so clogged in the upper sinuses that nothing comes out from the place where we have placed the voice. So don't be afraid to sing when you have a really bad cold. You will have a major breakthrough in your thinking about technique and the voice when you see what you accomplish and how wonderful the voice can sound even under bad conditions. Be careful, never strain, *sping* quietly first and then increase as you feel more comfortable and confident.]

Now don't get me wrong. I am not suggesting that you become a hermit. No, that is certainly not the intention. I am, however, cautioning you that if you do not take care of the instrument and treat it with kindness, tenderness and a great deal of love, it will quickly un-tune itself and not serve you in the way you expect.

Think of the violin again… sitting in its case for months, stuck in some damp corner. Just imagine its condition when it's finally picked up. And this is a man-made instrument. A few new strings and a careful tuning, and it's as good as new. Well, my dears, the voice is not like that—for obvious reasons. Everything you do, it does; everywhere you go, it goes; how you treat yourself has a direct bearing on the voice. So cherish your gift and consider it. Your emotions are a barometer for your voice.

I wish I had a dollar for every time a student came to me for a lesson really uptight about something that had happened during his day. It's quite a task to get the voice into place when you're in such a state. Everything that happens in your life is reflected in the voice. When you are happy, the voice is *up*; when you are depressed or strung out, the voice is *down*.

Obviously, if you are going to sing professionally, that cannot and must not be a factor. You must separate yourself totally from the rest of your life. When you sing, it's the voice and only the voice you think about. It's really tough in this hectic and highly-charged life-style we lead, but without a doubt— necessary. Anyone who shares your life must be aware of this, respect it, commit to it and understand it. If not, they do not belong in your life.

Perhaps until today (prior to reading this book), you may have given "the voice," the actual instrument and its workings, only a fleeting thought. Well, from this moment on, this must change. You have to accept the responsibility for your voice— technically, emotionally, physically, psychologically and spiritually. Before you read this book, you thought of the voice in a certain way, in one place. Now you will begin to perceive the voice in quite another way.

The road has been paved for you; all you have to do is follow. I pray you do—because unless you do, my mission in life will not be accomplished. At least not with you, and you are very important to me—each and every one of you. So spend your time wisely, search inside yourself and find the way. I have given you the tools, but the rest is up to you. I will repeat it again: have patience; allow the instrument to grow at its own pace. Don't push and don't go backward—trust and go forward.

chapter 15

The Career

This is not a book about how to make a career. I leave that in the hands of the management. My interest in the subject is purely directed at the voice.

I know you can sing, and I know you think you are ready for the "big time" and, perhaps you are. But consider a few things before you throw yourself at the mercy of national and international competitions and/or management. There must be preparation—not only vocally and musically—but psychologically and spiritually, as well. You will be pitting yourself against some strong competition, and you must be ready. Your whole being must be geared up for the events to come, and I'd like to give you some pointers that I've found helpful in preparing students and that I've observed while talking to many a singer at competitions.

1. Choose your repertoire wisely.

Consult with your teacher as to what repertoire you should prepare. Do not overstep your vocal boundaries. Stay with repertoire that may be a bit easier than what you think you can handle so what you are singing is exactly right for you and effortless. What's the point in showing off what you can do when the risk is so great? If you take on more than you can handle, it will only add extra pressure—and you surely don't need that. Prepare your Arias, or songs, with great care. Technically and musically—everything must be perfect. Think about sleepwalking. That's how you have to feel when you sing. When the music is in the voice and you are totally secure in what you are doing, you can step in front of anyone, at any time and be in control vocally.

2. Put the music into the voice.

Take your time in learning the music and the lyrics. Every note has to be put into the voice. You know how to do this: *Sping*, "EE" and then add the words to the music. You cannot just pick up a piece of music and sing it. No one who's really serious about singing can. The brain must be trained to give the body the right impulses, and that takes time. Not once, or even twice—but maybe twenty times or more. When you begin a piece of music, you're like a baby: first a helpless infant, totally dependent; then you learn to turn, to sit, to crawl, to stand, and finally to walk—then you're off. Putting music into the voice is along precisely the same line. When you begin (unless you are a genius) there will be many spots that seem out of reach. Patience, fortitude, love and lots of hard work will enable you to make headway every time you sing. The notes will place easier; the air will begin to flow freer; the *giro* will know exactly when to turn, when to cover (the natural cover is inside the *giro*); the brain will know how much diaphragm you need to sustain a phrase, where to take a breath and what the coloration of certain passages should be. The understanding and awareness of it all comes with thoughtful practice, patience and trust in the instrument and its functions.

Give your voice a chance. Don't push it into doing what you want. Follow its course, not yours. Work with it, not against it. Ultimately, you want the voice to win. Let it make a winner out of you. Respect the fact that the voice needs time to settle into a piece of music. You will see that sooner than you expect, the result you're seeking will be achieved.

Close your eyes often and hear the music inside your *third eye*. Visualize the movement of the system before you actually begin. Speak the music as though you were singing it. *Sping, sping, sping.* Your phraseology in speech is the same as in your singing. Always remember that. There is no difference. Place the speaking voice into the *soft palate* and on top of the *giro*. When you are *spinging*, measure the breath you need for the phrase. When you sing it, you will notice that it's exactly the same. Guide the breath always *upward* and "follow the yellow brick road" *up, back*, then toward the tips of your ears and the *bone of life*. You will see how powerfully you develop and what a profound relationship you will begin to have with your voice. Remember that wine is never sold before its time. So let your voice ripen; cure it and then offer it.

3. Be in control of your emotions.

Nerves are a big factor. If you were not nervous, something would be wrong. Everyone is and should be; however, a person is overly nervous when he is not sure of himself. If you have done your work and you have prepared, there should be no reason for you to be shivering before you sing. Nerves put you in touch with your vulnerability, and that is quite necessary. But use this to your advantage; feel it, experience it and make it into a positive, rather than negative thing. That's adrenaline, and you need it before you step on stage.

Dedicate the voice and ask for help. If you don't ask, you will not receive. Believe in your spiritual nature; allow it to lead you and trust it. Think of giving to those who listen to you. Think of enriching their lives with the beauty of your voice and know that with such great spiritual power behind you, you cannot fail. You will be calm and composed, leaving your fate up to the will of heaven. If the universe supports your efforts, you will be secure and in control.

chapter 16

Colleagues & Friends

In show business you get the gossip, pettiness and all of the other mean and rotten things you can think of. Scratch that thought. Forget it immediately. That's for the others; that is not for you. You can see all and hear all—but do not react. **Be proactive.** Think of your voice, your role, the music, the conductor, the staging—anything—but do not let yourself be sucked into intrigues. This is not what you want. Keep your opinions about other singers to yourself. Do your job. Be pleasant, cordial, professional, centered. Know who you are and be sure of your own worth; but don't be a snob. No matter how big you may become, remember that you meet the same people on the way down as you did on the way up.

Try to create only good feelings between yourself and others. Concentrate on being quiet and centered inside. Only then will you have complete control of the voice. Be friendly with everyone, but make friends with few. To be more precise, only make friends with the people that you have *tried* many times and that have proven their loyalty and sincerity to you.

Compliment sincerely, or be silent. Smile, but don't be false. Try to find the good in everyone and in every situation. Don't be aggressive. Be tolerant and assertive when necessary, but always stay within your bounds. Don't make waves. In the end it will not benefit your career. Being called a **diva** today is not always a compliment. Capriciousness and temper tantrums went out a long time ago. Look for harmony. Only in that way can you find yourself on the winning side. Don't be a wuss, either. Show character and know who you are; always stand your ground. Put the voice first. Think before you speak; the ramifications of your words create your future. Respect others, and you will be respected. Take a stand for yourself and for your voice, and you will see that others will begin appreciating you. It's important to look good, but don't sell your soul for it. Be an individual, but in all things, be circumspect, diplomatic and tolerant.

There is a great deal to be said for what we just discussed. In my years with professionals in the business, I have seen it all. I have also been witness to many a promising career ruined by all the superficial nonsense. So please, heed my advice and take care of your ego. That is really what it all boils down to, the ego. A healthy ego is good to have and is necessary in order to be able to step out onto the stage and give your best, but don't let it get the best of you. You can get more with honey than with vinegar… an old cliché, but really important when you're trying to enter the rat race of show business.

chapter 17

Speaking & Communicating

I have mentioned a number of times that speaking and singing are the same thing. If you learn to place your speaking voice in the same place as your singing voice, you will have an easy time of it.

Imagine if all day long you spoke in the throat as most of you do. You grate the voice and then all of a sudden when you start singing, you expect the voice to perform for you from another place altogether. It does not work. The system works equally in both cases, and you should begin visualizing your speaking voice in your singing voice position and vice versa. The more you are able to do that, the easier it will be for you.

I want to talk about communicating for a moment. Most of us do not think about it much, but as human beings and, of course, as artists, we need to spend time talking about this. Communication is such an important part of our lives. The way we communicate dictates how we are understood. Much is at stake. If there is a breakdown in communication, be that in interpersonal relationships or in the professional world, it is almost always due to some form of verbal misunderstanding. Whether we are speaking to a large group, expressing our emotions or just engaging in a normal conversation, our communication depends on our intonation, pronunciation, diction and the way we modulate our voices. Our voice reflects every emotion. Have you ever talked to someone over the phone and immediately, after the first hello, you knew that something was up? Of course, it has happened to all of us a hundred times. Our tone reflects our moods, and our words have an enormous impact on the people around us. With our speaking, we create our world; and it is in our speaking, that we open all the possibilities in our lives.

In my years of teaching I have developed a methodology of speaking with my students. I am very demanding as a teacher. I give a great deal of love, but I do not pamper. I demand the utmost, because I believe that is what it takes to be able to use the voice properly. A relationship must be built with affection, caring and mutual respect combined with a great sense of professionalism. I can teach a friend of mine, but while I am teaching, I'm the *teacher*, not the *friend*—and there's a major difference.

Even if a lesson is not going so great, and we are struggling, at the end of every lesson I compliment my student. Not to falsely make him feel good, but to acknowledge his effort. Sometimes, the student will be surprised by that and will say he felt he didn't do so well, or that the lesson was not successful. So I explain that every lesson, no matter how difficult, holds a key to his future success. In doing it wrong there is learning and an element of gain. Even if you don't think you got anything at the moment, the brain has absorbed the material. The brain will then compute the material; and perhaps, at a later time—when you least expect it—the brain will make it available to you.

Encouragement, acknowledgment and praise are necessary in developing communication with everyone. My students will tell you that I can really be tough, but at the same time, they will say that I give my all to that one note that ends up making the whole lesson worthwhile. It's the little things that count, the extras. Always be ready to step beyond yourself and go for the gusto. I do so in my teaching, in my life and in my dealings with others. I do not leave a stone unturned to help, as long as I see that the student is trying his very best. If I perceive a student not to be giving his all and feel that all of my effort is in vain, or if I feel that his heart and soul are missing, I let him or her go—with explanation, but I cut the cord.

Finally, it is all about humanity; and if I wanted to really get into this subject, I would have to write another book. But please consider humanity in all you do and allow that to be your yardstick in communicating with others. Sometimes things seem very black and white, but nothing ever is. Give the benefit of the doubt to everyone and think with your heart, not only with your mind. Most of all, be patient; please be patient. Patience is a great virtue, and the voice needs you to be patient and give it time to develop naturally.

Always talk to your teacher. Communicate. If you have something to say, say it. If you need an explanation, ask for one. Think about the system often and don't be afraid to address your fears. It's all part of learning, and a good teacher will understand and be open and honest with you.

Communication on every level is so important. Most of us go through life and have no idea of with whom we are dealing. We have friends whom we really don't know… and lovers, and siblings, and colleagues. Make an effort to give of yourself to others. Be open. I am not saying to tell everyone your life story, but in your dealings with family and acquaintances, be able to say what you mean and mean what you say. There is no point in playing games. Oh, I know—we all do it from time to time. It's expected. But try to limit this habit as much as possible. **Remember that with your word, you create your world.**

Honesty is not about hurting someone. It's about sharing with them how you feel and listening when they share with you. There are always two sides to every story. Always put the shoe on the other foot and see if it fits. You may think that you are right, but if you examine a bit more closely, you might see that the other party has a valid point, as well. Talk about it, and you will see that honesty and sincerity go a long way.

Did you ever hear the expression "the tone makes the music"? Well, that's the key. You can say almost anything to anyone as long as you say it in a way that they can understand. If a person feels your sincerity and genuine caring, he will not be angry with you when you say something he might not want to hear. Do not criticize, but critique instead; be constructive and kind; it's a whole different thing. Make sure that your points are valid, to yourself and to the person with whom you are communicating. Base your opinions on facts and on your feelings; but always be sure that your words hit their mark gently and with compassion. Talk to someone the way you would want him to talk to you. More easily said than done, I know. But please, pay attention: your ability to listen is imperative.

The ability or inability to communicate will be a major factor in your career. Your communication skills on stage have everything to do with how the audience perceives you. Pavarotti is a great communicator and so is Domingo. These artists have learned what makes us spectators tick, and they use it to their advantage.

A smile, a gesture, the way you stand, the look in your eye, the way you accept the accolades from the audience, your humility. All these important factors enter into how your future will map out. The generosity in your communication is important. Be large, giving, expansive and open. Don't hold back. Let go of yourself and share yourself.

Pavarotti, Domingo and Carerras are actually products of our hyped-up society. Oh, don't get me wrong. I'm not putting down their abilities as singers and personalities, by any means. They are communication masters on and off stage. They have done so much to make opera more broadly accepted and appreciated. They have sparked the imagination of so many and brought the Art to a wide spectrum of our society. They have made it exciting for us, and I applaud them as Artists and as humans.

I am just talking about the whole *image* thing. Let's take for example, Caruso and Gigli, Pons, Ponsel and Curci, Pinza, Chaliapin, Di Stefano, Gedda, Tagliavini, Tucker, Warren, Pierce, Bjorling and so many more. They were masters of the voice. Their names were not household words, except in the circles of opera and music lovers. None of them ever achieved the incredible popularity that the great publicity wheel of today has conjured up for the Three Tenors.

Alfred Kraus, who passed away just in the last days of editing this book, was one of the greatest artists of our time. He never sold out. His voice was his love, and his love for the instrument ruled his entire career. His later career was as glorious as his early one, because he kept the voice in the forefront of his dealings with the music. He never sang repertoire that was not indicated for his vocal abilities. He was a consummate artist and greatly respected for his personal and artistic integrity. But he, too, was not a *people's* artist; he was an *artist's* artist.

A pity that the general public did not learn to really appreciate his mastery, but that's the time in which we live. I believe that artistry and skill, stage presence and true vocal excellence will always be respected, revered and certainly never forgotten. Those singers will live on in our hearts, and when we talk of the **Greats** of Opera, it is to them that we are referring. Their communication to us bridges the information age, and so their recordings will live and inspire us forever. That is how they have touched our lives and hearts.

No one is perfect. We all know that, but the public wants to see only the best. So give it to them in all ways. The more you give, the more you will receive. I suppose that about sums it up. Open yourself to the possibility of being the best you can be and watch—the universe will support the noblest and highest thought to which you aspire. I wish it for you!

chapter 18

Sharing My Story

The voice has always played a powerful part in my life. I have always sung, and expression with my voice has elated me, satisfied me and connected me. Even as a very small child, music was a primary focus in my life.

I grew up in postwar Germany. Being Jewish, my life there was very difficult. My parents were concentration camp survivors, and most of the time there was great sadness in the house. Understandably so, now that I'm grown; but as a child, I did not understand that.

I had to find a way beyond all of the sorrow, so I turned to music. I remember taking my radio to bed with me, hiding under the covers and listening to music—not rock-n-roll, either—but operettas, opera and classical music. The voices of Marika Rock, Cornelia, Wunderlich, Caterina Valente, Rudolf Schock, and Richard Tauber (just to name a few) constituted some of my happiest listening memories. While listening to these beautiful voices (and other stars from all over the world), I would dream about being able to sing.

Well, I don't want to bore you with my trials and tribulations of not being taught properly and singing repertoire that was not for me (basically, all of the no-no's of which I've warned you); but when I was nineteen, I had my first surgery in the throat, and a few years later—I had the second. Vocal cords that have had nodules on them and have undergone operations will not perform for you unless you know how to position the voice properly. But I did not learn about that until it was much too late for me to think about singing again. Oh, I can still sing, and my students are always impressed with how I have reconstructed my own voice (my speaking voice); but very, *very* few have actually heard me sing.

Years ago I realized that for teaching, this is actually better. My students cannot emulate me. They cannot try to copy me; they have to rely on their own instruments. I cannot influence anyone with the brilliance and artistry of my voice—or with the fact that I've had a brilliant singing career myself. I have to communicate with words—giving examples, painting pictures, explaining details, sharing knowledge and using gestures, etc. I rely completely on my hearing and on my depth of understanding of the instrument. I am able to identify how and where a sound is made, how and why it is the way it is (cause and effect) and how to perfect it.

I give you what I know. I rely on my skill, my aptitude, my intelligence, my feelings, my instincts, my vibrations and emotions. I cannot rely on my voice. I have to communicate with words, and I have learned to do it in such a way that even a young child can understand the rudiments of the voice, follow my instructions and even do it!

Your vocal abilities are as personal as your individuality, and I am only a guide. So in a way, I am grateful for not being able to sing.

I never studied music formally. I have some basic idea from learning to play the piano, but I am self-taught. All of what I have shared with you here has come to me via spiritual knowledge, deep thinking, reflection and learning—from and with my students. I have not read the books of other experts of the voice; but as I mentioned before, I have worked with some great Maestri—not as an apprentice, but as a maestro myself, in collaboration.

I do not hold a degree from a conservatory, but have taught in quite a few. I realized many years ago that I was not meant to sing, but to teach. After a long and hard road, which took me to many parts of the world and thorough many personal tragedies, I finally accepted that challenge. With this acceptance came the information.

All I can tell you is that I know what I know and have the ability to do what I do because I am chosen to be the vessel that imparts this information to those who wish to know and accept it. *Birth Knowledge* is what I call it; the sum total of what I have learned and know from my past lifetimes. I know music that I have never heard before. I say words that seem to come out of nowhere, but the moment I speak them—they hit their mark. I sometimes marvel at what is coming out of me. I do not challenge my knowledge, I simply accept it and share it. I have taught voices that any other teacher would have given up on as lost, destroyed or unsalvageable. I take them on because I know that I have the capability of reconstructing them in the right place. My scientific colleagues, whom I respect sincerely, may not agree; but I have proven over and over again that it can be done.

I teach with the knowledge of being guided, and with the understanding that my own learning process is constant, and that I will be led to give to each individual student what he or she needs of me. I open myself up to them, and they open themselves up to me and together—we achieve their destiny, whatever that may be.

I do not take any credit for my knowledge. I am simply

grateful for it. I know that who ever comes to me and crosses paths with mine has a special spiritual lesson that has to be learned. This is not intended to sound pompous. Believe me, this is not an ego trip; this is simply what my experience has taught me.

I have been teaching for eighteen years. I've refined and honed my own skills so I can adjust to every student. It's like going to a doctor, except I treat the disease, the patient and myself. There are so many factors involved in helping a voice emerge. Sometimes we spend our time discussing the problems in a student's life. Why? Because they directly influence the voice.

I have no set lesson plan; whatever is necessary for the voice and its health and well-being is what I do. I follow my student's progress at his or her own pace, but under more or less normal circumstances, it takes about forty hours of study to put a voice together well enough to begin with repertoire. To completely finish a voice in all its nuances and get it ready for the stage takes between four and six years. If the voice is badly damaged, it will take longer; if the student is very instinctive, much less.

A great deal depends upon the spirituality of the student— what he wants to accept, how much of an ego he has and how much he will allow it to interfere with his progress. Openness is a key factor, and so is patience. I am not always successful. In the cases where I am not, I know that spiritual growth is not being achieved; I will send the student away if I am certain I cannot help.

I cannot teach if I do not love, or if I feel that ethically the student is not on a level where he can grow, both as a human being and as a singer. The voice is an integral part of you. It is you. Once you discover it, it will overcome you; and you will be able to achieve what you desire (if you use the proper tools, that is).

Your direction for singing must be there. You must know where you are going with the voice. I generally do not teach students who are very casual about singing, who really do not have a long term goal. I want the desire to share to be powerful enough to motivate. I do not teach students who are looking to be famous only for themselves, those who are only interested in becoming stars for the sake of fame and fortune. My students must want to give of themselves, to offer their voices to the Light and receive from the Light the guidance and the power to master the voice.

Perhaps you think me presumptuous. That's okay. Everyone has his or her own personal value structure, ethics and beliefs and above all, **integrity.** These are mine.

I choose my students not because they are going to be famous (because a great many will never be), but I search for what singing will do for their souls. With this in mind, we go on our journey to discover the voice. Incredible things happen when you discover the voice. Your life changes. Your outlook is broadened. Your personality takes on a whole new glow. Your self-esteem increases. Your confidence is strengthened. The voice is a tremendous source of power. One thing is for certain: I will not teach anyone for the sake of money. When your voice comes together, your life becomes whole.

I am, of course, remunerated for my work. In our society, unfortunately, we need to be. I say "unfortunately" because if I could, I would teach for free. I would go anywhere in the world and spread my teaching and give it without thinking about how much it costs to get there, to stay in the hotel and to buy the food, etc. It's my dream, and who knows? Perhaps, one day it will happen. I was able to do this in the Ukraine and in

Russia when there was no money. I taught for food and lodging and the pure joy of doing what I do best. This was one of the greatest personal and professional experiences of my life. I shall never forget the voices that touched me, and the ones that I touched.

During the hour we spend in a lesson together, you own me. I give you all I have; I empty my vessel. When I finish, I am depleted yet elated. What I in turn need for my student to give to me is his or her enthusiasm, love and trust. Without that, there is not the exchange of energy that is necessary in order for me to teach. After I finish with you, I have to give to someone else; so if you only deplete me without giving back to me, I cannot fill up again. What I am talking about is a constant recycling of energy and a refilling of the vessel, a constant search and acceptance of the Light into our teaching relationship.

About a year ago I was in a music store looking for some Arias for my students. I do not ever read material on singing. I am generally not interested, except for one time; and I would like to share that experience with you.

Every so often a student will bring me a book. I will glance at it and put it down again. They are usually too complicated for me, or too involved, too scientific, too many words that cannot be understood by a lay person. I know what I know and do what I do. I do not look to copy others or to compete with them in any way.

Anyway, as I was browsing through some musical scores in a music store, I noticed something very out of place that definitely did not belong in the musical scores section: a very small book entitled, *Hints On Singing*, by Manuel Garcia.

I had no idea who he was. I do not know, really, why I

picked it up or why I thought it was familiar… why the name stirred something in me. I opened the booklet, leafed through and read a line that mentioned the spoon. I got the chills. I read some more. The book is basically questions and answers. I bought the book and quickly read it. I found such incredible similarity in our methods that I felt that perhaps, here was the connection for which I had been looking. I do some things quite differently from him, explain the terms in my own words (most of which you have read). I have refined my own methodology, but some of the real bread and butter basics are the same. Other very important segments are completely different—like some of the terminology that I have coined and now use, etc. But on the whole, it fascinated me, and I wanted to find out if there was some connection.

Coincidences? I don't think so. I don't believe in them. *Birth Knowledge*? Yes, only that makes sense to me—a past life connection, without a doubt. I know that everything in my life has brought me to this point.

I share my knowledge with you because I have to, because I have no right to keep it to myself. The more you give, the more you get. The more open I am to sharing, the more the Light will provide. So I ask you to partake, but please think about giving it back. Only in that way can you, too, become a vessel that continually fills itself and has a never-ending capacity for giving.

It turns out that Manuel Garcia is considered the greatest voice teacher that ever lived. He created a dynasty, but very little is written about him. His son Manuel Garcia II wrote the book I read. Manuel Garica's wife, Joaquina Garcia, and I share the same birth date. Try to find information about him. Perhaps, you will have more luck than me. I was able to find out very little, but I know that there is a spiritual connection between us.

Recently someone has come into my life and through astrology, has found other similarities that connect us. I trust my instincts—the voices inside of me that know, and I am grateful that I was the one chosen to disseminate this information to you.

I hope that I have enlightened your life, that I have shared the Light with you, that you will gain the right use of your voice and confidence, happiness and success through what I have tried to impart to you. I invite you to contact me and share with me.

appendix

The Drawings

An Overview

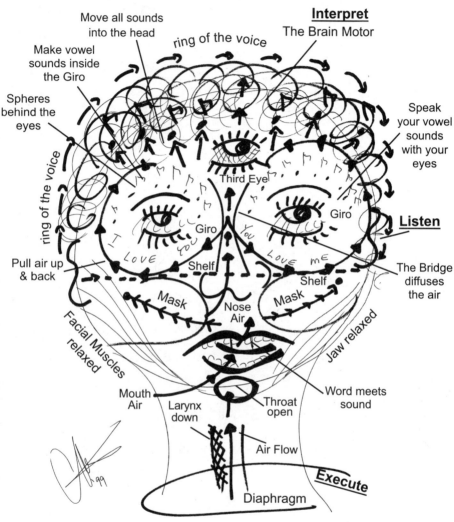

Interpret
The Brain Motor

Move all sounds into the head

ring of the voice

Make vowel sounds inside the Giro

Speak your vowel sounds with your eyes

Spheres behind the eyes

ring of the voice

Third Eye

Giro

Giro

Listen

Pull air up & back

Shelf

The Bridge diffuses the air

Shelf

Mask

Nose Air

Mask

Facial Muscles relaxed

Jaw relaxed

Mouth Air

Larynx down

Throat open

Word meets sound

Air Flow

Execute

Diaphragm

1) Breathe simultaneously through mouth & nose
2) Lead the air up & back past Hard Palate, Uvola into Soft Palate
3) Soft Palate pulls up & back, lifts & stays lifted at all times
4) Pull air from mouth as far back as possible toward Bone of Life, open hole
5) Air from nose opens Chamber & allows the Giro movement

6) All sounds are formed in the back
7) Air remains in the back to make sound & move the Giro
8) Intention of word moves sounds over the top of the Giro toward Third Eye & angles to the lips.
9) Sound & word (diction/ consonants) meet at the front teeth & lips & exit together
10) Allow the brain to be the motor of the voice & let the Third Eye visualize the entire movement

Appendix: the Drawings

The Voice Part 1

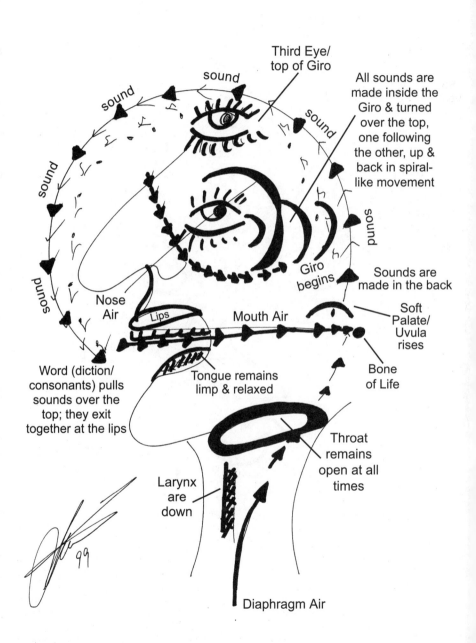

Third Eye/ top of Giro

sound

All sounds are made inside the Giro & turned over the top, one following the other, up & back in spiral-like movement

sound

sound

sound

sound

sound

Giro begins

Sounds are made in the back

Nose Air

Lips

Mouth Air

Soft Palate/ Uvula rises

Word (diction/ consonants) pulls sounds over the top; they exit together at the lips

Tongue remains limp & relaxed

Bone of Life

Larynx are down

Throat remains open at all times

Diaphragm Air

The Voice Part 2

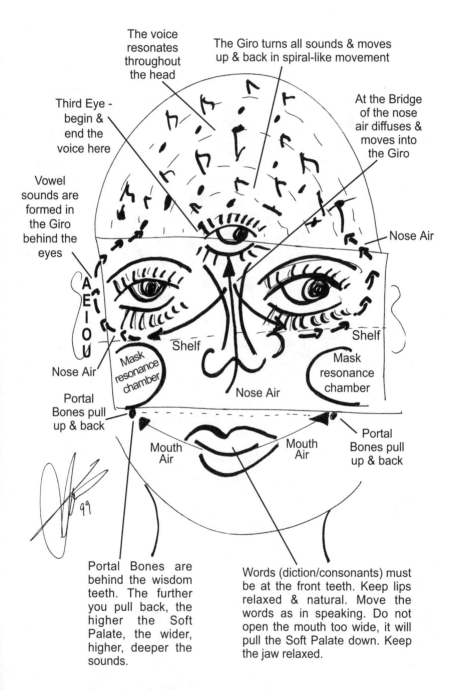

The voice resonates throughout the head

The Giro turns all sounds & moves up & back in spiral-like movement

Third Eye - begin & end the voice here

At the Bridge of the nose air diffuses & moves into the Giro

Vowel sounds are formed in the Giro behind the eyes

Nose Air

A E I O U

Nose Air

Shelf

Shelf

Mask resonance chamber

Mask resonance chamber

Nose Air

Portal Bones pull up & back

Nose Air

Portal Bones pull up & back

Mouth Air

Mouth Air

Portal Bones are behind the wisdom teeth. The further you pull back, the higher the Soft Palate, the wider, higher, deeper the sounds.

Words (diction/consonants) must be at the front teeth. Keep lips relaxed & natural. Move the words as in speaking. Do not open the mouth too wide, it will pull the Soft Palate down. Keep the jaw relaxed.

The Voice Part 3

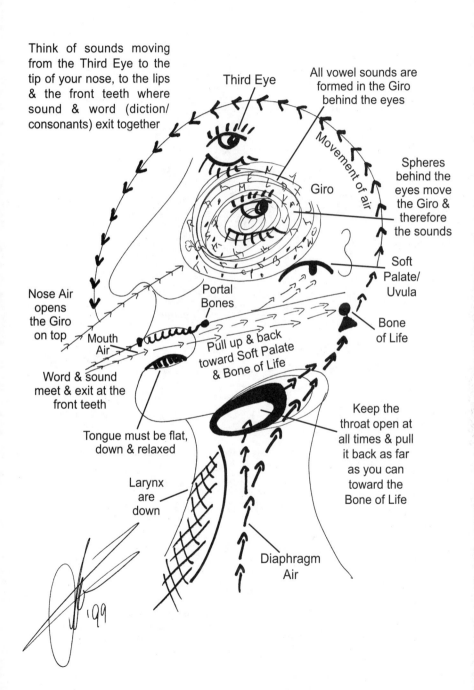

Think of sounds moving from the Third Eye to the tip of your nose, to the lips & the front teeth where sound & word (diction/consonants) exit together

Third Eye

All vowel sounds are formed in the Giro behind the eyes

Movement of air

Giro

Spheres behind the eyes move the Giro & therefore the sounds

Soft Palate/ Uvula

Nose Air opens the Giro on top

Portal Bones

Bone of Life

Mouth Air

Pull up & back toward Soft Palate & Bone of Life

Word & sound meet & exit at the front teeth

Keep the throat open at all times & pull it back as far as you can toward the Bone of Life

Tongue must be flat, down & relaxed

Larynx are down

Diaphragm Air

'99

Air Movement

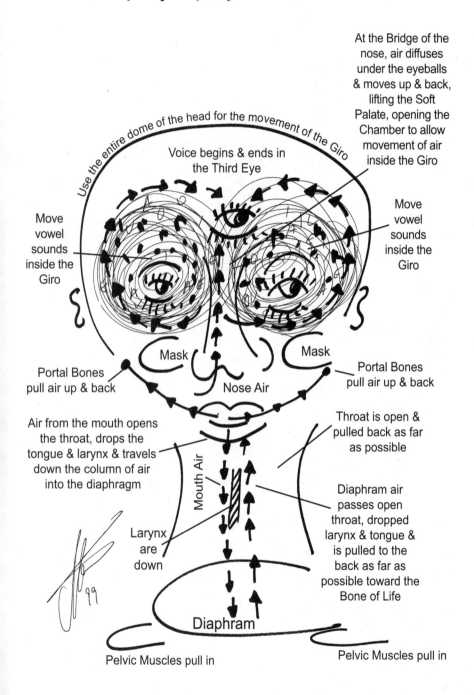

At the Bridge of the nose, air diffuses under the eyeballs & moves up & back, lifting the Soft Palate, opening the Chamber to allow movement of air inside the Giro

Use the entire dome of the head for the movement of the Giro

Voice begins & ends in the Third Eye

Move vowel sounds inside the Giro

Move vowel sounds inside the Giro

Mask

Mask

Portal Bones pull air up & back

Portal Bones pull air up & back

Nose Air

Air from the mouth opens the throat, drops the tongue & larynx & travels down the column of air into the diaphragm

Throat is open & pulled back as far as possible

Mouth Air

Larynx are down

Diaphram air passes open throat, dropped larynx & tongue & is pulled to the back as far as possible toward the Bone of Life

Diaphram

Pelvic Muscles pull in

Pelvic Muscles pull in

Lagtime

The second between creation of sound in the back, turning of the Giro & exit of the sound at the lips is **Lagtime - the single most important movement in keeping the voice on the top**

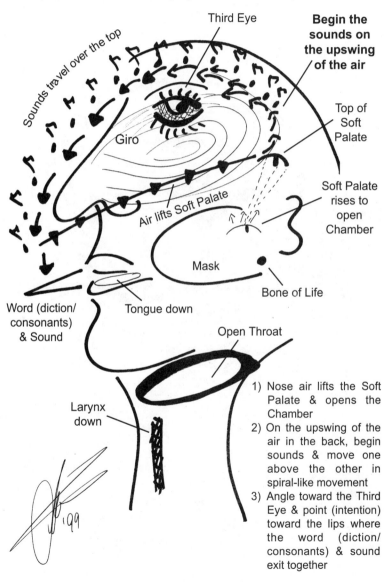

Third Eye

Sounds travel over the top

Begin the sounds on the upswing of the air

Giro

Top of Soft Palate

Air lifts Soft Palate

Soft Palate rises to open Chamber

Mask

Bone of Life

Word (diction/consonants) & Sound

Tongue down

Open Throat

Larynx down

1) Nose air lifts the Soft Palate & opens the Chamber

2) On the upswing of the air in the back, begin sounds & move one above the other in spiral-like movement

3) Angle toward the Third Eye & point (intention) toward the lips where the word (diction/consonants) & sound exit together

Movement of the Vowel Sounds

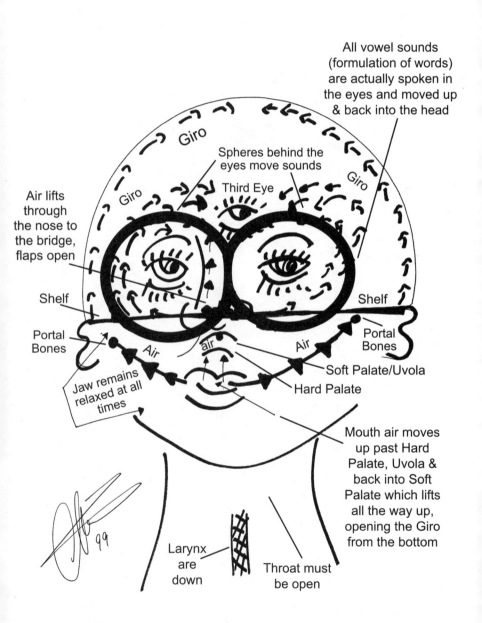

All vowel sounds (formulation of words) are actually spoken in the eyes and moved up & back into the head

Giro

Giro

Giro

Spheres behind the eyes move sounds

Third Eye

Air lifts through the nose to the bridge, flaps open

Shelf

Shelf

Portal Bones

Portal Bones

Air

air

Air

Soft Palate/Uvola

Jaw remains relaxed at all times

Hard Palate

Mouth air moves up past Hard Palate, Uvola & back into Soft Palate which lifts all the way up, opening the Giro from the bottom

Larynx are down

Throat must be open

Three Sources of Air for the Giro

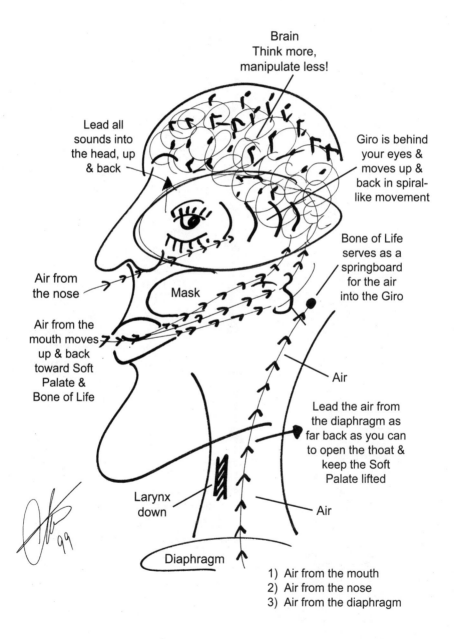

Brain
Think more,
manipulate less!

Lead all
sounds into
the head, up
& back

Giro is behind
your eyes &
moves up &
back in spiral-
like movement

Bone of Life
serves as a
springboard
for the air
into the Giro

Air from
the nose

Mask

Air

Air from the
mouth moves
up & back
toward Soft
Palate &
Bone of Life

Lead the air from
the diaphragm as
far back as you can
to open the thoat &
keep the Soft
Palate lifted

Larynx
down

Air

Diaphragm

1) Air from the mouth
2) Air from the nose
3) Air from the diaphragm

Last Note Front View

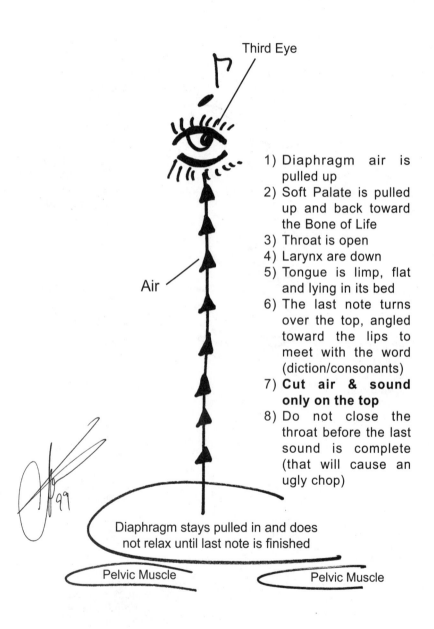

Third Eye

Air

1) Diaphragm air is pulled up
2) Soft Palate is pulled up and back toward the Bone of Life
3) Throat is open
4) Larynx are down
5) Tongue is limp, flat and lying in its bed
6) The last note turns over the top, angled toward the lips to meet with the word (diction/consonants)
7) **Cut air & sound only on the top**
8) Do not close the throat before the last sound is complete (that will cause an ugly chop)

Diaphragm stays pulled in and does not relax until last note is finished

Pelvic Muscle   Pelvic Muscle

Last Note Side View

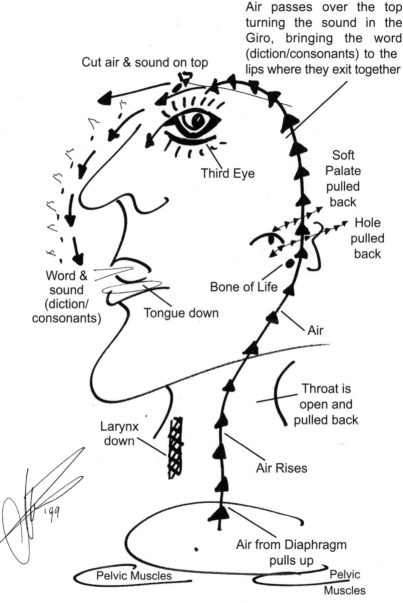

Air passes over the top turning the sound in the Giro, bringing the word (diction/consonants) to the lips where they exit together

Cut air & sound on top

Third Eye

Soft Palate pulled back

Hole pulled back

Word & sound (diction/ consonants)

Tongue down

Bone of Life

Air

Larynx down

Throat is open and pulled back

Air Rises

Air from Diaphragm pulls up

Pelvic Muscles

Pelvic Muscles

1) Diaphragm is pulled all the way in and held there
2) Soft Palate is in up & back position & remains there
3) Sound must turn over the top, angled toward third eye & front teeth & meet the word (diction/consonants) at the lips
4) Air & sound must be cut on the top, not in the throat

Glossary of Terms

Glossary of Terms

BRAIN IMAGING: Brain imaging is almost like visualizing and is done practically in the same way—in the *third eye*. Basically, we project a picture in the brain of how we visualize the process of the movement of the air: the turning of the *giro*, the pulling back of the *portal bones*, the lifting of the *soft palate*, the opening of the throat, the dropping of the tongue. We image the movement of the pelvic muscles and the pulling in of the diaphragm. We project the dropping of the larynx, the opening of the throat and the flatness and relaxation of the tongue. All this occurs in a split second, before you sing a note. If you want to, you can *brain image* at your leisure, at any time, really. It's great to put your head on a soft pillow in a dimly lit room, close your eyes and watch the whole thing in front of your eyes like a movie. Only in this movie—you are the producer, the director, the lead actor, the gofer, the makeup artist and the scriptwriter. It is your movie, and you are in control. As you design it, so it shall be. If you design it with all the elements we have learned, your *brain imaging* will be a powerful component in your total progress; so do it often and be very precise in your projections.

BONE OF LIFE©: The most important focal point in the back of the throat. If you focus the air from the mouth all the way to the *bone of life* and use that position as a springboard for the *giro*, the voice will be properly balanced in top and bottom vibrations. By pulling toward the *bone of life*, the maximum extension of the *hole* is achieved; the throat is *open* and allows the air to come *up* from the diaphragm and support the height of the *soft palate*. All of the components in technique pull in the direction of the *bone of life:* the *portal bones*, the *soft palate*, the air from the diaphragm, the *hole*, the sounds in the *giro*. In other words, this is a one-way street. Everything moves *up* and *back* toward the *bone of life,* the *top of the giro* and *into the head*.

DIAPHRAGM: The motor and support system of the voice. Air is moved (past the *open* throat, *dropped* larynx and lowered tongue) *down* the column of air into the diaphragm. By contracting the pelvic muscles, you pull the air back up through *open* throat, *dropped* larynx and lowered tongue to support the *soft palate* in its *highest* position. Use the diaphragm a minimum of three times: the first note, the highest/lowest note and the last note—and every note in between.

THE EYES: The great movers of the sound. Behind your eyeballs, the spheres move the air of the *giro* and, therefore, the sound. You must learn to actually speak your vowel sounds *inside the eyes* and make the word in the same place. Only in this way is the line of the sound secured. If you drop the word (if you speak the words with your mouth and under the *portal bones)*, you will lose the roundness and brightness of the sound and fall into the throat.

The eyes are the mirror of your soul, and your soul is in your voice. So speak *with your eyes,* and you will always be in position.

GIRO: The *endless loop* of the voice, THE PLACE where the sounds are made; it *turns* on a continual basis, round and round; each sound follows *over the top* of the other, exiting at the *third eye,* angling toward the front teeth to exit with the word.

The bottom of the *giro* is the *soft palate*, and the *top* is the *third eye*. It is imperative that all sounds are made inside the *giro*. The *giro* moves *up* and *back* only (never downward toward the throat, always, *upward* into the head) and is moved strictly with the air. The *giro* can be big or small, depending on how high or low the note needs to be. The size of the *giro* determines the depth of the voice and the coloration of the sounds.

The further you pull *up* and *back*, the higher, the larger and the darker the voice will be.

LAGTIME©: The time it takes the air from the NOSE to enter at the bridge of the nose and diffuse the air under the eyes (the shelf). The air has to be pulled all the way toward the back, lifting the *soft palate* to its maximum and creating the **chamber** in which the *giro* circulates. All the sounds you will ever need to make are within the *giro*. The sounds move to the back, and the intention of the word (diction) pulls the sounds over the top to the front teeth and allows them to exit together. *Lagtime* separates sounds (in the back) from word/diction (in the front). It keeps the voice *on the top* and *turning* properly inside the *giro*. It is the single most important movement to keep the voice *on the top*. There must be a split second time difference between the making and turning of the sound and the coupling with the word. If there is not that *lagtime*, word and sound will both start in the back. If that happens, the *soft palate* collapses, the throat closes and the voice falls into the throat. (Please read chapter 5 many times to familiarize yourself with this concept.)

PORTAL BONES©: These can be found by placing both thumbs at the end of your top teeth, just beyond your wisdom teeth. They are round little bones that you must think of pulling *backward* and *upward*, in order to move the *soft palate* into the *up* and *back* position. The *portal bones* are also the guideline for the sound. No sound should ever be made below that place, and if you are making words below the *portal bones* (which is a no-no), the voice will fall into the throat. Visualize the pulling *back* and *up*, and you will find that you can move the tissue around the *portals* along with the *soft palate*.

SPINGING©: Speaking and singing in the same position. *Spinging* is achieved by placing the air all the way on top, *behind the eyes* and moving the sounds in a circular motion inside the *giro*, while pulling further and further *back* with the muscles of the eyes. (Visualize the movement of pulling, and the brain will do this for you.) The *higher* and the further *back* you *sping*, the more flexibility you will develop inside the movement. The deeper the *sping*, the larger the *giro;* the larger the *giro*, the more color in the voice, hence, the more possibilities for enlarging the sound. The spheres of your eyes move the sounds and *spinging* will make sure that you are always in the correct singing position: *behind the eyes,* moving *up* and *back* at all times. *Sping* a great deal before you begin singing. Please, although it may sound like a fire engine to you, you must believe me: learning how to *sping* is invaluable in the growth of the voice. Use only sound, at first; then attach vowels to the sound and then add the words. After the breath pattern is established, *sping* the melody and tempo of the piece you want to sing, exactly. Then put melody and "EE" together. After that feels completely comfortable, add the melody plus word. You are teaching the brain the movement of each individual note, so pay attention and do it right; otherwise the brain will learn it incorrectly, and it will be very difficult to unlearn.

THIRD EYE: The beginning and the end of the voice. Here the *giro* places the sounds at the end of the turn; from here, the sound angles toward the word (diction/consonants), which occurs at the front teeth and the lips. The *third eye* helps you *visualize* the exact place where the sounds are, and your ability to achieve a total spiritual opening to the voice depends on it.

VISUALIZING: The brain is the great coordinator of our whole being, so the voice and its production are no exceptions. The more internal the conceptualization of the technical aspects of the voice, the more in control the brain will be; thus, the more out of control you will be. The less you physically assist the voice, the better it will be. The more you allow the voice to find its own natural place, the more familiar you are with the instrument and the less you seek to manipulate it—the more it will serve you. The work we are doing is internal, not external. No pushing, forcing or pulling on the jaw; no drastic facial movements. Visualize the sound, the place, the *giro*, the head, the *bone of life,* the words *inside your eyes* and the vowel sounds behind the spheres of your eyes. Feel more than you usually do and breathe life into the sound. Allow the voice the freedom to exist in its natural habitat. Be the guide, but not the maker. Trust your instrument and your singer's instincts and follow what we have already talked about.

Vocalises for All Voices to Begin With

- Work your way chromatically up the scale, in your range, **legato** - turning inside the Giro

- Start with *MEE*

- Continue, adding different vowels to different consonants

Miriam
Jaskierowicz
Arman

about the author

Miriam Arman was born in Postwar Germany to Concentration camp-surviving parents. She immigrated to America in 1962. Educated in the U.S.A., she has taught privately and in Master Classes in Israel, Italy, Hungary, Romania, Poland, the Ukraine, Mexico and many other places around the world. She has been involved in all phases of the music industry, from management to production to directing for television and on stage. After spending 11 years in Europe, she returned to the United States in 1996; and in 1998, she founded the *International Academy of Voice and Stage Inc.*

She has been passionately involved with the physiology of the voice for 30 years and for the past 18 years, has dedicated herself exclusively to teaching. In 1984 she began her in-depth research and studies with Italian voice teachers and musicians: At **La Scala di Milano** with Maestros Tonini and Baracchi, at the **Teatro Regio di Torino** with Maestro Fogliazzi, and with Maestro Daniel Chain at the Conservatory in Milano.

She is fluent in six languages. Her particular specialties are the Italian *Bel Canto* repertoires and German *Lieder*. She teaches privately, in Master Classes, and lectures and conducts special seminars throughout the world. Ms. Arman is also a noted international fine artist

How to Get in Touch

To order materials, please send a certified check or money order in the amount specified to:

Music Visions International
P.O. Box 17345
Plantation, FL 33318-7345

Materials currently available*:

- *"The First Lesson"* with Miriam Jaskierowicz Arman, Cassette - **$9.95**; CD - **$15.95** plus **$4.95** shipping and handling.
- *"The Master Class"* video with Miriam Jaskierowicz Arman, **$24.95** plus **$4.95** shipping and handling.
- Additional copies of this book, **$14.95** plus **$4.95** shipping and handling.
- All drawings and cover available in 18"x24" posters, signed by artist Miriam Jaskierowicz Arman, **$24.95/ each** plus **$4.95** shipping and handling.

    *quantity orders available

Orders may be e-mailed to **voiceacad1@aol.com** *or see our website* **www.nvo.com/greatvoice**

Teacher Apprentice program available. For Master Classes, workshops, lectures or seminars with Miriam Jaskierowicz Arman please contact: **Music Visions International**